HOW TO MARKET AND SELL LIKE A PROSTITUTE

Proven and practical ways of making people buy your products or services, even when they do not love you and your company

EDWIN NGWANE

Rights Reserved.

© 2019 Edwin Ngwane

No part of this book may be reproduced or transmitted in any form or by any means, electrical or mechanical, including photocopying and recording, or by any information storage or retrieval system without permission in writing from the author.

Disclaimer

This book is written for informational purposes only. It was not written to glorify prostitution or demean those who practice it. The words prostitute, prostitution and sex are used just as references to marketing and selling. The author has made every effort to make sure the information is inspiring and educative. All attempts have been made to verify information at the time of this publication and the author does not assume any responsibility for errors, omissions, or other interpretations of the subject matter. The publisher and author shall have neither liability nor responsibility to any person or entity with respect to any loss or damage caused or alleged to be caused directly or indirectly by this book.

Author's Guarantee:

The author of this book researched his subject and provided enough insights to help someone who is having challenges with marketing, branding, and selling. Please contact us at +260 965 208 410 if this book does not help you in any way. We will not hesitate to refund you.

ABOUT EDWIN NGWANE

Edwin Ngwane, CEO of Kawiwi International Limited, is a writer and public speaker. He has authored *"The Few Who Find Gold"* and *"The Wedding Master Plan."*

Ngwane teaches others how to transform their lives into greatness by achieving entrepreneurship, sharing with students his background of living in the village and the middle class.

Ngwane is a graduate of the University of Mysore in Karnataka, India, where he acquired a Bachelor of Commerce. He is now a seasoned banker with management roles in sales, customer service, and banking operations.

Ngwane is married with two girls. He can be contacted through LinkedIn, Twitter, Facebook and Instagram under Edwin Ngwane.

DEDICATION

How to Market and Sell Like a Prostitute is dedicated to all entrepreneurs and would-be entrepreneurs. Your ambition to pursue risk with a positive attitude is what drives economies, creates wealth, and changes lives.

ACKNOWLEDGMENTS

Edwin S. Ngwane (Grandpa)

For giving me the first capital to start a business.

Mwika Manda

For showing me all the street marketing and selling techniques.

Astrida Mwila

For being a supportive wife, even when I lost money through failed businesses.

CONTENTS

Chapter One: YOUR BUSINESS IS DEAD WITHOUT SALES 16

Chapter Two: BECOME SHAMELESS AND BELIEVE IN YOUR BUSINESS 25

Chapter Three: FIGHT OBSCURITY AND GET YOUR BUSINESS OUT THERE......35

Chapter Four: FIND YOUR NICHE AND BUILD YOUR BRAND............46

Chapter Five: DON'T SELL TO THE UNCONVERTIBLE................59

Chapter Six: DEVELOP A SERVICE CULTURE 72

Chapter Seven: MAKE THEM FALL IN LOVE WITH YOUR PRODUCT...........81

Chapter Eight: OBSERVE THE MARKET AND LEARN NEW TRENDS.............91

Chapter Nine: CLOSE AGGRESSIVELY AND UNAPOLOGETICALLY 100

Chapter Ten: SPEAK TO THEIR MIND AND SOUL................115

Chapter Eleven: RIDE AND GRIND LIKE NO OTHER................127

Chapter Twelve: BREAK THE RULES AND BE READY TO FIGHT............136

Chapter Thirteen: BUILD RELATIONSHIPS.................153

Chapter Fourteen: LEVERAGE ON THE NEW CROP OF PROS............ 168

BACHELOR OF ARTS IN MARKETING AND SELLING AS CERTIFIED BY THE STREET AND CORPORATE WORLD

I was introduced to street selling in 2006 by my good friend Mwika Manda at Lusaka City Market. We were selling secondhand clothes. There are two types of secondhand clothes sellers: bulk sellers who open bales and retail sellers who collect designer clothes from the bulk sellers for resale.

I was a re-seller of collected designer secondhand clothing, which was known as a "Vocal." We used to select the best secondhand clothing, selling them to those who loved Italian, English, American and French designs. The clothing was sold at a fairer price than it would cost had it been bought brand-new.

Our business model, therefore, was basically about understanding fashion trends. We collected the latest and stylish clothing, selling them to the people who loved fancy clothing at affordable prices. Business was always good once you understood fancy clothing and knew to whom you could sell the clothes.

Due to financial constraints, I started this business after having to survive after not attending college. I became an expert in the business and was in love with the vocal business.

I could tell whether the bale had nice designer clothing, even before it was opened. I was well-educated about brands sold within H&M,

Dolce & Cabana, Gucci, Paul Smith, Marks & Spencer, Old Navy, Gap, Zara, American Eagle, Abercrombie & Fitch, etc.

The vocal business became my business. I was certified by the School of Vocals. It taught me the language, behavior, negotiation skills and appearance of vocals. Vocal basically meant someone who could talk and persuade someone to buy. I was part of the tribe of vocals, and I am still a proud vocal to this day.

I did not understand how much I had learnt about prospecting, networking, building rapport, and credibility, or closing and relationship management until I joined the corporate world of banking in 2009. I was asked to sell something to the interviewer on the day of the interview.

As a vocal, I could even sell my shoes and go home with sandals! I aggressively sold my jacket to the guy who asked the question. He wanted to buy my jacket - a solid British wool retro style with notch lapel. It was the best jacket in my wardrobe, but money is money. I sold it to him and got the job.

On joining the bank, my first position was Direct Sales Representative (DSR). We were the bank's foot soldiers. We would walk from one door to another in the central business areas of Lusaka, looking for clients. I was never afraid of this challenge since I had already been a vocal.

Many people couldn't handle this type of work. It was the ladder for me, however, and I used it to become one of the high-performing managers in the corporate world of banking. Even though I thrived, direct selling is not an easy job.

I remember reading sales books written by Brian Tracy, Jeffrey Gitomer, Daniel Carnegie, and others. I began to understand all the sales processes. After studying these guys, I realized the important elements of selling. Still, I felt something was missing that I needed to understand.

I began to study colors when I started my restaurant business. I wanted to understand why fast food companies branded their buildings with red, yellow and green. I was intrigued as to why blue, teal and green were common among financial institutions. My research went further by revealing to me why most advertisers use mothers and children in adverts.

At the same time, I still wanted to know someone who is the master of sales. Grant Cardone claims this title in his book — *Sell or Be Sold*. He is aggressive and pitches like no other. What about the marketing gurus like Frank Kern or Russell Brunson?

I bought and read their books, learning valuable lessons in the process. However, I wasn't satisfied. There is something all these guys talked about in relation to learning something new.

They would encourage you to 'model successful people' who are already where you want to be. Therefore, I started looking around for people who had mastered the art of marketing and selling. I started to look for people who could market and sell a product that is not morally acceptable yet commonly sought and bought.

I like to go out to a party once in a while so that I can have fun with my friends. You will meet me one day. We tend to visit a few night clubs here and there, spending some time on the dance floor. I am that guy who likes to dance, despite having limited dancing skills, though I can jump.

After going out for a while, I noticed one common trend at night. Guys look for women for either a one-night stand or whatever. This is not an envelope statement. Some guys also used to go out just to dance, talk about sports and politics, or make business deals.

This statement is also true for women. Not all women found in night clubs are prostitutes. They tend to go out for fun. But there are those who go out for business. These are the types who don't hide the fact that they make money through having sex.

Studies have shown that married men buy sex more than single men.

This statement alone created a lot of curiosity in me. I wanted to understand why a married would go out there and have sex with a prostitute. I just couldn't comprehend that. After making concrete observations, I learnt how prostitutes HUSTLE at night to get money out of men's pockets.

They don't get it by force. They don't steal (although some do). Men willfully pay for the services rendered. And guess what? They pay a premium for services, which can be acquired for free from their beloved wives. Instead, they decide to get these services from someone they do not even love.

Upon looking at the whole picture, I studied how prostitutes do their business. I realized that they are masters of the marketing and selling game. Few men can proudly say they love prostitutes, despite having acquired their services at some point in their lives.

Prostitutes sell a product, which is morally unacceptable, demeaning, risky of infections and illegal in most countries. Furthermore, they sell to both men of lower and higher ranks within society, which gives us the opportunity to learn their selling techniques.

We can learn how to market and sell our products to people, even though they do not love our company or the people running the company. I believe every business is dead without sales; therefore, it is paramount to understand how to get your products and services to the people who are eager and willing to buy.

This book was not written to glorify the work of prostitution or demean the people engaged in the business of prostitution. Instead, it is designed to use the prostitutes' principles of client acquisition and retention, marketing and sales in the world of business.

I hope this book will help you widen your market reach, boost your sales and increase your revenues.

Enjoy.

Chapter One
YOUR BUSINESS IS DEAD WITHOUT SALES

If you do not strive to market and sell your business, then overall, it is dying. People provide advice about money and how it should not impact the day-to-day operation of a business. This business mindset, in fact, is foolish.

Businesses can survive without money, but the killer of most businesses is the lack of money. Money is the oil that runs a business' engine. Therefore, you need to learn how to market and sell products. You cannot discount marketing and selling if you want to become a millionaire, for marketing and selling is the gateway to earning money.

After working six years in the corporate world of banking, I quickly realized I would not be a millionaire just as an employee. So, I looked at all the dynamics of employment and thereby understood that an employee is not in control of his income destiny.

An employee gets only a fraction of what his employer thinks he is worth. The executive sits and discusses the organization's performance, deciding how to reward employees after the shareholders (rightly so) have gotten their lion share. The average salary increment within most business circles is 5-20% unless you move from one salary scale to another. Typically, this is due to a promotion or a change of an organization.

While moving from one company to another in an effort to search for greener pastures, you will still notice that an employee of lower ranks earns an income to keep him going.

I analyzed someone earning a gross annual salary of USD18,000.00 while getting the average annual salary increment of 10 percent. This usually depends on the performance of the employee and the organization. The expected compound annual salary s/he will achieve over 20 years will be USD121,094.99.

I soon realized that I would not be a millionaire working for another person, despite working my butt off all year round. So, I slowly started working on my side hustles.

In 2011, Chikondi Beauty Care was established. The business was a great start-up in the small town of Chililabombwe. Miners' wives bought our beauty and cosmetic products.

Chikondi Beauty Care did very well and overgrew quickly; however, it collapsed in 2016 when I was transferred from Chililabombwe to Ndola. Upon arriving in Ndola, we used the concept of Chikondi

Beauty Care but did not market research the potential customers within the city.

We believed the concept of targeting ladies who enjoy looking good would work in the city. We opened Chikondi Beauty Care under the new names of Chikondi Charms. The shop was painted with beautiful purple colors. The branding was on point, and the display sparkled.

We stocked our store with high-quality perfumes, deodorants, wigs, hair oils, nail polish, boxers, bras, panties, and pieces of jewelry. My wife and I felt great just having the products in our shop. However, the business went under sooner rather than later. I lost all the money I put into the business, which took five years to pay off. It was painful, and I was angry with myself. I thought I had it all figured out.

I thought people would buy our products, and, therefore, we would make a lot of money. The reality is that business teaches great lessons. I was beaten to the game, learning great lessons about marketing and selling in the process.

I like to read. One day, I saw an article written by Victor Antonio, which read: "Everyone is in the business of marketing and selling." And it's true. You can have the best products and/or services. Still, they aren't the best, and you are not in business if you can't sell your products and/or services.

If you are not getting any traction and generating money, you should look for a different job. Running a business is not for you. There is no business that can survive without generating sales.

Apple, Amazon, Coca-Cola, MTN, and Trade Kings are massive companies that have not made a mistake when it comes to marketing and selling. Coca-Cola is gigantic, but they have never stopped marketing and selling their products and/or services. If big companies can market and sell their products and/or services, then a small business like yours needs to double its efforts.

The failure rate of a start-up business is at 75% during the year of its inception, 97% in its second year and 99.9% in the third year. The biggest challenge for most start-ups is cash flow through which sales are made. Having said this, it becomes very difficult to keep up with the operating costs of the business if the products and/or services are not being sold.

In my book, *The Wedding Master Plan*, I pointed out that a beautiful woman with a noble character can still fail to find a partner. This is especially true if she lacks certain marketing and sales tactics. It's why you find businesses selling crappy products and making money, all while your great business is struggling to sell quality merchandise.

The problem is not the country's economy, just as it's not the price or the product's timing. Instead, you lack the practical marketing and selling techniques essential for a successful business.

You can spend a lot of money on packaging and reducing prices, though your business will soon fail if nobody knows about your products and/or services. I know a lot of businesses who liked to compete on the basis of price, but they ended up being annihilated.

You don't have to reduce your prices. How are you going to sustain your business with reduced income? How are you going to pay employees and stakeholders with reduced prices? Where is the money going to come from for innovation?

You might also think that there is nothing you can do about your country's bad economy. But remember, there is someone with a business just like yours. They are killing it and making money in your industry. You can do just as s/he can do it.

The worst mistake you can make is to believe people haven't any money. People are always buying things. It's false to assume that people don't always have money. The prospect doesn't think about you when making the decision to buy.

I remember sitting on a bench at Lusaka City Market, thinking that someone would look at my fancy clothes. They would buy them because they were nice. It was a bad move, and instead, I ended up broke. I hadn't earned any money until I became a real vocal.

I started talking to prospects, showing them why they needed to buy a faded blue damaged pair of American Eagle jeans. It had buttons instead of a zipper. Further, I explained why beige embroidery was better than black for blue jeans. Customers need to understand that. Without specifying the jeans I was selling, the pair was just another item of clothing they could find elsewhere.

Whenever I wasn't speaking with prospects, I would complement those wearing a fancy suit at a restaurant. They ended up telling me where they bought their jeans, and I would mention I could provide similar products at a suitable price. These are selling tactics I used as a vocal, but I failed to use them when I opened Chikondi Charms.

I became too comfortable being an employee. Thus, I didn't do what could have made my business a success. I was that corporate guy—the one who thought it was awkward to pitch perfumes, wigs, nail polish and jewelry.

There are so many people who hate selling. In fact, selling is one of the most disliked jobs in the corporate world. But there is a secret: "numbers don't lie." A salesperson in employment circles finds it easier to justify their performance and rewards for this reason. Even in business, the company which is selling products looks like one. A good-looking bottom line usually comes from a strong top-line.

Learn how to sell if you want to become successful in your career. Every company wants someone who can move their products and/or services to the consumer. Jobs are always there for you if you are a good salesperson, and the corporate ladder is easier to climb.

Marketing and selling, therefore, is an integral part of business success. Sales revenue is the engine that drives a business. So, you must learn everything to thrive with marketing and selling.

What is marketing anyway?

According to the Merriam-Webster Dictionary, marketing is defined as: "the activities that are involved in making people aware of the company's products and/or services, making sure that the products and/or services are available to be bought."

The other definition of marketing is: 'the action or business of promoting and selling of products and/or services, including market research and advertising.' The business dictionary defines marketing as: 'the management process through which goods, products and/or services move from concept to the customer.'

What is selling?

Selling is part of the whole concept of marketing, as you can see from the above-mentioned definitions. The main goal of marketing, therefore, is to move products and/or services from the business owner or salesperson onto the customer.

The Cambridge Dictionary defines selling as: "the activity of making products and/or services available so that people buy them." It further expands the definition as: "the job and skill of persuading people to buy things." I love the way the Cambridge Dictionary expanded the definition. You should go through that definition again.

Marketing and selling is the hardest part of a start-up business. I see so many entrepreneurs getting everything right, except for putting a sales team in place. How are you going to let people know you have great products and/or services? You need to advertise this message way before you launch your business.

The resources are usually limited for most start-up businesses. Still, you can win by using the concept of the prostitutes. While studying your competition, offer something they can't imagine seeing. This will get their clients' attention, and they will watch.

Your market research needs to match your products and/or services to the needs of your clients. Complete a SWOT analysis before you throw yourself to the wolves. Every business will face stiff competition in the beginning. Thus, you have to prepare adequately and fight for your market share.

Prostitutes understand this concept very well. Think about it. Men don't like prostitutes, but they certainly love what they offer. They are magicians who know how to turn a boring day into an exciting one. And once a man falls for their magic, he needs better magic to go back.

I have flirted enough, and it's time to go deep. I believe you deserve to know what makes prostitutes sell a product that should not be sold, especially being in one of the most despised industries around the world.

Turn to the next chapter, and let's begin.

Chapter Two
BECOME SHAMELESS AND BELIEVE IN YOUR BUSINESS

The first time I did a sales job was when I was employed by Standard Chartered Bank, working as a direct sales representative (DSR). Friends or relatives would give me advice on finding a decent job once they heard of my occupation.

It was very frustrating, but considering I came from the street, where I sold secondhand clothing, it didn't bother me. This made me realize that a sales job was not a respectable job for many people. I now understand why many people left the sales role. Even if they left for a mediocre job, it was not sales.

Nonetheless, my observation has been that most successful executives and entrepreneurs are great salespeople. They will sell a vision to the workers, financiers, relatives, clients, and many other stakeholders on their way to success.

Sometimes, the sales pitch might seem trickery or crooked, which is why most people shun away from selling. There are so many people with great products or services who fear being rejected or looking like a scam. If you can't put your product and/or service in people's hands, then you are doing a disservice to yourself and/or your business.

You are someone who lacks value and is weak. There are so many people who can acquire help from your product. Still, you have insecurities, which have made you fail to share these with the people.

THE 5 THINGS STOPPING YOU FROM SELLING

Fear of rejection

The fear of rejection arises for most people when it comes to sales pitches. No one wants to pitch a product and/or service only to get rejected. We all want people to agree with us. But the world is a little different from what your mother taught you. It's brutal! People will reject ideas, even when they are good for them.

I am sure you have an ego on your shoulders. You think it's not right for people to reject your products or services. Leave your ego at home and go out there. Get rejected as many times as possible until it stops hurting whenever someone says no.

Fear of failure

Failing is not a good experience. Failing makes people look stupid. I remember being mocked by someone who owned a shop near our place on the day I closed *Hot Grill Takeaway*. He thought it would be easy for me, but then I faced reality.

I was embarrassed when I failed to pay workers' salaries. It was painful to explain why you couldn't pay someone who worked tirelessly for your business. There were days I wished I didn't open the restaurant, but rather just used the money to get a BMW. I regretted having tried to work as a business owner.

Nonetheless, after a few months or a year, I realized that having tried and failed to run a business gave me enough lessons for future use. I learnt great lessons, which I won't make in my next business. I became wiser by understanding why I had to go through it.

I know you are afraid to sell your products and/or services. You are fearful that you cannot persuade buyers to make the purchase. At one time, you may have felt the pain of criticism toward your products and/or services, or experienced failure to succeed with a new item that you thought would be successful.

At the same time, you must be willing to fail if you want to succeed in business. It is all a game of chance. Sometimes, it works; sometimes, it sucks. You will learn great lessons if you are willing to go through the process with an open mind.

Fear of criticism

When Jack Ma started Alibaba, the Chinese e-commerce website, people criticized him. They said he was promoting the sale of fake products. 2pac was criticized for his gangster rap until he became a rap legend.

Jose Mourinho has been criticized for being talkative and winning through pragmatic ways. I remember seeing people criticize Donald Trump until he became POTUS. Moreover, people criticized Jesus Christ for surrounding himself with prostitutes and thieves. Look at his ministry now.

Every new idea, concept, product and/or service will be criticized. Someone said you should say nothing, do nothing and be nothing if you don't want to be criticized. Is that what you want for your life? I don't think so.

Every great book has bad reviews. Every great song has people who hate it. Furthermore, what you consider flavorful food may not look or taste good to others. We live in a diverse world. It's important to recognize that not everyone will love you or like what you offer.

Develop a thick skin for criticism. Allow people to criticize you and your products. You might even benefit from the criticism if you listen well.

You think your products or services are not good enough

Ask people to tell you about themselves, and they will be conservative. They will try to hide their achievements and accolades of what they have achieved in life. Most people want to appear as underachievers. Who gave you such a mentality? It hurts me to see people with such a mindset.

If we were to meet, you would encounter a guy who is handsome, intelligent, successful and in the process of becoming very wealthy. I am the full package of God's creation. I am a talented author, speaker and business coach. This book is a success even before I publish it. It's a bestseller.

I couldn't care less about what you think. I am the master of my own fate, the captain of my soul. I think, speak and do what is good for my life. Everything I do is a success. You are free to disagree with me, but I really don't care. This is the mindset you need to have.

If you do not believe in yourself, then it will be very difficult for someone to believe in your products and/or services. You don't trust yourself enough to believe you can create something spectacular. You think it's impossible for people to accept what you sell.

Why do you think people will reject your products and/or services? Do they understand the amount of effort you have put into your business, as well as the time it takes to bring them to the marketplace? It's okay if they don't see the value.

You are good enough, just as the items you sell are good enough. If the Chinese could flood Africa with junk and make a killing out of it, then why would you think your products are inferior?

You are too good to be a salesperson — Ego

Most people can be anything but a salesperson. It's a job that is disdained in most communities. But the good news is that selling will be the last job to be replaced by technology. So, your MBAs will not amount to anything if you don't know how to sell in the future.

You think you are running a business, yet you have more important things to do than selling. It's no surprise that your business is struggling. If this is your mindset, then I can tell why your job is on the line. You will be laid off soon.

Nobody is too good to be a salesperson. Whether you are an Evangelist, prophet, business owner, executive or just another guy trying to find love–you need to learn how to sell. Salespeople are very attractive people in business, careers, and life in general.

Successful sales professionals get more promotions. In fact, they are usually higher paid than non-sales professionals. You will also notice that the marketing and sales departments are the most important departments of all corporations.

Most successful people and corporations have sold products, services and/or ideas in order to become successful. Steve Jobs, Mark Zuckerberg, Bill Gates, Jeff Bezos, Kylie Jenner, and Oprah Winfrey have all sold something to become successful. Learn how to market and sell if you want to be like them.

You have set a low target for your life

A love affair with contentment is common among those who don't enjoy selling their products and/or services. Salespeople stretch themselves to achieve more. A Toyota Corolla, a two-bedroom house and two children on a government scholarship is good enough for those who have given up already.

But good enough has never changed the world. You have to look beyond the wall. See the possibilities beyond what your eyes can see. You can do and become more. You deserve more than what you have. I know you are capable of getting what you want for your life.

I don't want to be a parent who leaves nothing for my children. I will leave an inheritance for my children's children. I want my grandchildren to live a better life because I laid a solid foundation for them.

There is nothing wrong with having more money; this is a good thing. Being very rich is also a good thing, for it allows you to buy more cars and fly more jets. What is stopping you from acquiring more? This is the same bullshit thinking that money is evil.

Read the scripture once again. The love of money is the root of all evil and not money itself. You have just settled for the low life, and so you are probably secretly praying for a breakthrough. Just learn how to sell. Only then will you will see the abundance, which will help improve your life.

You think marketing and sales is for extroverts

It is common that most people think a salesperson is always pushy, overconfident, outspoken and aggressive; however, this is not always the case. Some great salespeople are down to earth and soft-spoken.

We live in a technological world, where you can advertise products and/or services through social media and Google Ad Words. Overall, this technology has made it easier for people to do great things in their lives.

If you are an introvert, then remember that there are other introverts out there just like you. They would love to do business with someone who is just like them. We sell more by creating meaningful relationships. You are in the right business if you are someone who likes to dig deep before you can sell.

The world of introverts has arrived. You can market and sell without talking too much, trust that it can be done.

PROSTITUTES CASE STUDY

Prostitutes don't care about what anyone thinks about them. They will stand in the streets looking for business, even though they know that most of the people passing by look down upon them. They are fearless, determined, and focused on what they want.

Prostitutes are shameless. They are so focused on what they do that they don't hear anything bad you say about them. It's a tough and challenging business, but somehow, they know how to do it better than most people who have a master's degree in marketing.

Prostitutes think having sex with them is the best experience someone can ever have. They persuade a man to have a better sexual experience instead of the boring sex he gets with his wife. This type of confidence is infectious. You can easily pass it on to another person or customer.

No one will have confidence in your products and/or services if you doubt them yourself. It will show in your business, and you will increase my fears of buying from your company.

No one will resist your product and/or service if you believe it first. We will be attracted by your passion, confidence, and admiration of your products, so much so that we will justify your business to those close to us. We will tell them how the product and/or service have improved our lives.

In actuality, there is nothing new that prostitutes offer their clients. Their belief is that having sex is a great experience. It makes potential clients think it is worth trying. Most men wonder why they spent all their money on five minutes that didn't seem any different from what they could have had with their wife.

As I previously mentioned, most married men leave their wives for prostitutes. Men believe they will get something spectacular; however, it ends up not being any different. This is what happens when you believe in your products and your business. You can sell sand to the people in the desert if you believe in yourself and your products and/or services.

Chapter Three
FIGHT OBSCURITY AND GET YOUR BUSINESS OUT THERE

There is a common phrase throughout business circles about career advancement, which implies it's who you know that matters. You need to know somebody if you want the next job.

Even though the previously mentioned phrase is frequently used, I don't agree with it. There is some truth in it, but it's not correctly phrased. The phrase shouldn't be about who you know, but instead, who knows you. We all know a lot of people, but the few people known by POTUS end up millionaires or successful business owners. Therefore, it is ultimately a game of who knows you.

Do you remember the old adage about publicity? Donald Trump used to talk about it often before he became POTUS. There is no such thing as bad publicity because all publicity is good publicity.

When I was studying my Bachelor of Commerce, I enjoyed one topic in particular, which was positioned marketing. Simply put: it is the way of making the customer think about your company whenever they think about certain products and/or services.

All toothpaste is Colgate in my country. Throughout America, people think about smartphones–especially iPhone. And, upon visiting Africa, you will almost think a vehicle somehow means Toyota. There was a time when computer operating systems only meant Windows.

What does this tell you about positioning? It simply means these companies have made their products and/or services well-known to their consumer. Customers think about the company as they think about a particular product and/or service. The way Coca-Cola advertises, for instance, gives you the impression that Coke means thirst.

Look at how Nigerians market themselves. Certain people in America and Europe think every African is Nigerian. It is so simple. After branding, positioning and advertising yourself as a company, customers will start shopping your products and/or services.

I am sure it happens to you with supermarkets or restaurants. Food is not always Wendy's, KFC or McDonald's. Coffee is not always Starbucks. Hollywood is not all about movies. Still, that's how our brains operate at a subconscious level, whether we like it or not.

Therefore, it is paramount to ask how you can position yourself. This will allow you to dominate your potential client's mind, making it easier to persuade them into thinking about the type of products and/or services that you offer.

Let's return to thinking about prostitution a bit. Prostitutes like to go to places known for pickups. They go to streets known for their picking up of prostitutes. If there is a college known for young prostitutes, then even the old prostitutes would find a way to get there.

Whenever someone thinks about having sex without creating a meaningful relationship, a prostitute often comes to mind first. In fact, people in any town will tell you where prostitutes can be found. It is usually a certain street, night club, guest house or Lodge. They may be found in a hookup line or on a particular website.

Prostitutes register their presence in all these areas so that they can increase their chances of getting a client. They are known by taxi drivers, hotel guards, bartenders, DJs and waiters. They don't hide their products and/or services, but instead, it is common knowledge for all.

You have to get known, regardless. People don't easily buy from unfamiliar people or companies. Most people hate window shopping. I am a guy who likes to search the web for the best e-commerce sites. These sites sell certain products I'm interested in, and I get settled once I find the best one. I can confess that it's not easy to settle for a site.

You have to check for the contact details, reviews, whether the site is verified by Visa, etc. It's hectic. This is why people settle for Amazon, eBay, Alibaba, or Etsy. It's because it's not easy to find the right supplier or seller of a certain product and/or service.

Now that we've discussed the importance of becoming well-known, read through the following steps designed to help you.

1. Advertise

Think about it. If a company like Coca-Cola can advertise, then aren't you supposed to do it a million times more? You have to advertise. You just have to do it, whether it's on television, radio, billboards or social media.

It takes five times for an advert to make an impact on a prospect. You will not make any money if you are not willing to advertise. You have to consistently push your products and/or services to the customer. I don't care how much money you are going to lose in the process. It's better to lose money advertising than patiently waiting for the death of your business due to your failure of not advertising.

If you don't want to spend money, then do word-of-mouth advertising. You have to be shameless! Talk about your business everywhere. Some people won't like it, but they will surely talk about it. In fact, they will still end up promoting your business.

You are not realistic if you think adverts don't work. All top brands you recommend to others are due to advertisements–these companies advertised to you first. In retrospect, you have been promoting their products and/or services to your friends and relatives ever since you came across them.

You probably have that one radio or TV advertisement that you love while you joke about it with your friends. You found the product and/or service, thinking you should try it. So, in retrospect, you are now an evangelist of the company.

It works if big companies can consistently do it. Try it for your own business.

2. Network. Network. Network.

One of the first things you will notice about a night club is that prostitutes are usually in groups or teams. They have this type of friendship, which helps them to get clients.

Prostitutes use their networks to support each other, giving one another a confidence boost. This is in case their friend is afraid or feels like quitting. They also use it to pass one client to their trusted friend if a client comes, but the prostitute is already preoccupied with someone else.

Who is in your circle? My grandfather used to say that "birds of a feather flock together." It is in your best interest to surround yourself with people similar to yourself. As a result, you will become a better business person by being surrounded by people who understand your mission.

3. Get into the spotlight

Do you hate the spotlight? Do you feel it's better to take a back seat in life? Do you like bragging every time you talk about yourself and your business? Do you feel as if fame is not a good thing? Are you afraid of speaking on stage?

If you answered yes to any of the above questions, then you need to consider coaching to become a real go-getter. My mum would tell you that I never talked and have always been a reserved guy.

Although it did not help me in any way, people would get into my stuff, and I would just let it be. If people wanted to get in front of me, I used to let it go. I then realized we are in a jungle, where you have to fight for what you deserve. I had to start demanding what was rightfully mine.

Let me tell you a secret. Any person who is well-known commands a certain type of respect in society, even when he is a fool. The guy who speaks will look intelligent, even when there are quiet guys keeping their brilliant ideas to themselves.

The well-known prostitute gets more business than the unknown prostitute. It is what it is—hate it or love it. No wonder most prostitutes love the night club's lights or stand near street lights when they are in the streets.

They want potential customers to see them while not wanting to cast doubt about what they do. They leave their house and get into the spotlight. As I previously mentioned, you have to stand firm to criticism when you are in the spotlight.

Have you seen the number of adverts during the FIFA World Cup or Super Bowl? Do you know how much it costs to have your advert on TV during those times? You should contact an advertising agency for a quote. Business is all about attention. The business that gets the most attention is the business that will thrive.

4. Dress to attract

Does a mini-skirt or being half-naked do any magic? Yes and no. It works for prostitutes but not when it comes to business. If you look at a prostitute, you will not have to ask whether s/he is selling sexual pleasures.

The clothes will tell you the whole story. Imagine going to a chemist and finding the pharmacist dressed in oily mechanic clothes. Would you buy the medicine or consider visiting the next chemist?

I can almost predict that you will not be comfortable buying medicine from a pharmacist who looks like a mechanic. You would still have question marks on your face if you found a guy sitting in a garage looking like a Chase executive banker.

It's the same with business. You should know your business dress code so that you don't make people doubt your credentials. I know your mother told you never to judge a book by its cover, but people do. Get used to it.

5. Create Controversy or Polarity

The easiest way to become famous is to create controversy around a particular topic. "Build the wall." — Donald Trump. "Jews are our enemies." — Hitler. "I can make angels visit our church right now." — Prophet Bushiri. "Social media is good for our children." — Gary Vaynerchuk.

The sentiments above are debatable issues, which offer perspectives from different types of people. Not everyone wants the wall. Not everyone thinks Jews are their enemies. You can't say angels came to your church just to make a TV stunt. And not everyone would love kids to have access to social media.

Some people strongly agreed with those sentiments, while others rejected them with their passion. These are what you call "polarized views." Controversial or polarized views will get 50% of the people supporting your idea, while the other 50% will be opposed to you.

Still, it is the easiest way to get known by your clients. It doesn't always work, however, especially when you are trying to demean or ridicule other people. This method has worked many times, so find a way of making your products and/or services a little controversial.

While the title of my book could have been *How to Market & Sell Like a Professional*, I know professionals are bored with the topic. Therefore, inserting prostitute into the title brings out many questions.

I know some readers will not be amused by my use of the word prostitute, but I am unapologetic about it. We all know you need water to quench your thirst. Likewise, beverage companies have made you believe you need a drink instead of water. So, therefore, create your own intelligent controversy.

6. Endorsement

An endorsement is one of the most visible types of getting credibility as a new business, especially when you want new customers. I am sure you have seen Lionel Messi with Pepsi.

A celebrity, sportsperson or otherwise well-known person will attract certain types of customers to your business. Overall, their feelings toward the influencer reflect how they feel about your products and/or services.

Influence marketing is a new trend right now. People with a million followers on their social media channels have set prices to talk about your products and/or services.

You might be thinking that it is expensive to get endorsed or that the ROI is not guaranteed. On the contrary, imagine what would happen if your business (whose target market is teenage girls) was endorsed by Ariana Grande.

7. Location and Accessibility

One of the biggest mistakes I have made in business was where I opened my store. Do I open it upstairs or inside an alley of the building? I used to make these decisions based on finances. While I would justify this decision in the past, this is no longer the case. I want my businesses along the road.

I mentioned before that prostitutes are usually found along a certain pickup street, night club, guest house or lodge, hookup website, etc. They make it easy for potential customers to approach them. Just imagine a respectable potential customer approaching the wrong person.

Prostitutes know how important locations are and how these locations affect the sale of their products. This clears objections out of the way before the customer thinks or talks about them.

Make it easy for your clients to buy your products and/or services. If your business is located at a lodge outside town, then creating accessible ways of making your customer is necessary. Make sure the elevator works if your business is on the fourteenth floor because your business is not a gym for clients to come and exercise.

The other way to create easy accessibility is by using online platforms. Before I launched my podcast, *Business & Money*, I wanted to open a full-fetched radio station. I was tired of going to radio stations; however, I came to realize it was a waste of money and time.

I share my story using platforms like iTunes, Stitcher and Google Play. As a result, I reach more people internationally.

If you don't advertise your business, then your product and/or service may likely be a failed business idea. Take your business idea out there and make it reach people.

It is not up to you whether people like your products or not. Just believe in what you are offering and tell someone else about it. Remember: people buy from who they know and the companies that advertise.

There is some metric behind marketing and selling. If one million people know you, then only half of those people will like you. And guess what? Only one percent of the people who like your business will buy from you. This means that your magic number is 5,000!

Following the mathematics above, we might say we need more people to be aware of our business, products and/or services. This gives us a chance to sell to them. Remember: you are already in deep trouble if no one knows you or your business exists.

Get known!

Chapter Four
FIND YOUR NICHE AND BUILD YOUR BRAND

If you are in business, you've probably pondered the best type of products or services to offer your customers. It's tough to come up with a business idea. The biggest temptation would be trying to sell what everyone else is selling.

So many people succeed by selling generalized items within their businesses, but it's not the right way to do business. This is especially true if you are a startup. Imagine if you are a teacher who provides classes. This is like providing classes to pupils from grades one to 12.

It appears as if you would have a lot of pupils to teach; however, overall, you will not build a brand worth its recommendation. You should be known for your brand, for people will refer to you in this way. Mark, for instance, teaches grade nine mathematics while Jennifer prepares biology examinations for grade 12.

Teaching grade nine mathematics is a niche market for Mark, just as preparing biology examinations for grade 12 is the niche market for Jennifer. If they both do it for more than three years, they will both be considered experts. They will become masters!

Look at football clubs. Almost every club has its own tradition and brand. Arsenal has a beautiful free-flow football; Bayern attacks with eleven men, and Barcelona are the pioneers of the tick-taka style of play.

There are different niches to music as well—hip-hop, country, pop, contemporary, rock, heavy rock, and/or classical. Within those categories, you will find artists who write music, parental guidance and gospel. That is known as niche and brand.

HOW TO FIND YOUR NICHE

Now that we understand the importance of creating a niche business, it is time we look at ways in which you can find a niche for your own business.

Self-awareness

The first step to finding your niche lies in the ability to know yourself. Who are you? What is it that you can do easily without frustration? Every human being was born with a God-given talent. This gift is something that can change the trajectory of your life once you know and learn how to use it.

The secret to knowing yourself is the ability to listen to what people say about you without letting them define who you are. Dig deep within yourself to find the gold which the almighty God has put inside you.

Look for problems your talent can solve

The world is full of problems. But guess what? Opportunities will arise in those problems. People are always looking for solutions. It is an entrepreneur's job to find a solution and make money while proving it.

If people are complaining about the lack of hospital health care, create a business that focuses on patient care. Offer that product and/or service to premium hospitals. While people are complaining about patients' health care, you can create your own niche by offering proper care. This has nothing to do with what nurses and doctors do but offers patients new health care options.

Study your competition

The good thing about business is this: competition is easier to beat when you focus on your niche. A lot of companies do multi-products and/or services, to the point where it becomes expensive and tedious to do the 'small stuff.'

Bigger companies tend to stop paying attention to certain aspects of a business with a lower ROI. And again, this becomes your opportunity! It's like being hungry and having an opportunity to sit under the king's table. I would be surprised if you were still hungry.

The king cannot eat all the food that is put onto his table. Kings, queens, princes, and princesses tend to be wasteful. They will refuse to eat certain types of food for fun reasons. It is your responsibility to study what they don't want to eat and aggressively go after those crumbs.

Balance money and passion

The worst scenario in this whole concept would be going after a niche-your passion. It is a product and/or service for which people are not willing to buy. Remember that the whole point of writing this book is for people to be able to buy your products, even when they do not enjoy you or your company.

At the same time, they should love your products and/or services. Your products and/or services should be amazing for people to buy. I do not subscribe to the "follow the passion and not money" bullshit. You should definitely love what you do, but you MUST make money while doing it.

There are so many passionate and talented singers, footballers, artists, producers, dancers, writers, speakers, etc. All their talent went to waste because they couldn't balance passion and money. You should put all the mechanisms of making money in place before you even think about becoming passionate.

Find a niche within a niche

If you try to do too many things, very few people will take you seriously. Therefore, you need to narrow it down to finding your niche market. Find a niche within a niche if possible.

1. **10 businesses and examples of niche markets**

    1. **Photography** — weddings; advertisements; graduations; portraits; music videos.
    2. **Home Essentials** — butchery; vegetable shop; toy shop; flower shop; clothing boutique.
    3. **Fitness** — women's gym; yoga; weight loss; dance gym; jogging club.
    4. **Garage** — Japanese cars; German cars; scooters; sports cars; truck garage.
    5. **Author** — romance; business; finance; start-up; theology; witchcraft.
    6. **Supplier** — office equipment; fire extinguishers; CCTV cameras; food.
    7. **Entertainment** — horse racing; squash club; rugby; cricket betting; dance club.
    8. **Clinic** — surgical; optical; children; home care for elderly people; dental; Gynecology.
    9. **Public Service** — political; religious; inspirational; philanthropy; entertainment.
    10. **Media** — PR services; news; entertainment; education; reality.

Let your customers know your products — don't confuse them.

You can easily find a niche within a niche after reviewing the above-mentioned niches.

More are listed below:

1. Luxury wedding photography; sports cars; advertising; photography.
2. Butcher knives; fruit market; red rose boutique.
3. Big women's yoga; elderly men's jogging club; perfect body classes.

I do not need to go till the 10th point, for I know you understand how to extract a niche with a niche. It is what makes you become an expert in your field.

Invest in your business

I have a passion for working in the restaurant business. I believe it will be my core business for a long time, thereby diversifying myself to other types of businesses. There was a fast food business I admired when I started my business. In fact, I competed with this business for a while because of its committed clientele.

Despite having all the business and committed clients, this fast food business continued in the same building without renovating. That is until innovation closed them down a day at a time.

New restaurants were offering free Wi-Fi, sports entertainment, a kids' playgrounds for kids, and new chairs and tables. There was beautiful artwork and colors, while this business only offered country music on a small speaker system.

How can you make more money like that? It costs money to make more money. You have to be willing to spend money if you really want to be in business for an extended period. Look at how prostitutes polish themselves with fancy clothes, brand-name shoes, and expensive perfumes. They understand what it takes to get business. You have to look and walk the part.

Business-related costs, e.g., equipment, building expenses, advertising and/or taxes, uniforms or technology, will never come cheap for you. Coca-Cola spends billions each year on advertising, while motivated staff keeps the company afloat. Still, all these companies need money.

A business that doesn't spend money will eventually close its doors. The new generation will consider the business old-fashioned; therefore, it's vital that you analyze how to make your business grow. It will become more profitable and appeal more to the consumer.

The survival of any business depends on how clients perceive you. You are in deep trouble if they don't perceive your business well.

BUILDING A BRAND

The first thing business owners should do is build a brand. You have to decide on the type of business you want to have, thereby additionally choosing which type of products and/or services you will be offering. You will not be the type of business that does everything. General dealing is wrong for business.

You should be known for something. Apple products are known for great designs and a premium price. Mercedes-Benz has been trusted for years as a luxury sedan. Adidas has provided sports clothing to people who have loved their brand for a long time.

Let me tell you why a brand is crucial for both marketing and sales. You probably have a brand that you defend and protect. In case you don't agree with me on that, then consider this thought. Have you seen how BMW and AUDI drivers debate about the superiority of one car over another?

If you do it right, that's how the customer will be defending your products and/or services. They unconsciously market your products and/or services to their family and friends. Isn't it a nice thing to have a brand?

STEPS TO BUILDING A BRAND

1. Know your target market

Prostitutes don't target every type of guy. They target their ideal clients while putting all their energy into getting noticed. They dress, speak, behave and network like their target clients.

Don't try to get everyone on board as you build your brand. Create your own tribe of clients, who will follow you like a cult. If you target a certain type of client and speak their language, then overall, they will worship your products. They will preach to everyone about the greatness of your products and your business.

2. State your WHY.

You will fall for anything if you do not have the WHY for doing something. Ultimately, you will not go anywhere if you do not have a reason for doing what you do. Therefore, you need a purpose; you need to have the WHY.

Some companies put their WHY in their mission statements. Others put their WHY in their slogans and taglines. Nike tells its clients to "Just Do It." America tells its citizens to believe in "liberty and the pursuit of happiness." These two examples mean something for both Nike and the American people.

Your WHY will define WHAT and HOW you do. Your WHY will guide you. It lays out the culture for your people and your clients. Your clients will love you for it, as it will separate you from the cloud. It will make your clients feel proud to be associated with your products and/or services.

Your WHY will make you stand out.

3. Model brands in your niche

If you look at smartphone manufacturers, they all talk about the camera and speed of their operating systems. Some talk about capturing the night sky, while others talk about capturing your beautiful moments. Night photography targets those who love sophistication, while beautiful moments go to people who appreciate events.

All the same, the bottom line here is the camera. Whether they talk about Android or iOS, we all know that what is cardinal to the process is their phone's operating system. It is important to look at what your competitors are marketing and creating. Create something similar but also uniquely different.

Don't try to reinvent the wheel. You can come up with something different from your competitor but focus the product and/or service, specifically to the needs of your brand. Look at Facebook, Instagram, WhatsApp, and Twitter. They are all social networks with some similar features but still different in how they function.

4. Create a resonating logo and tagline

Hip-hop musicians love Gucci, and Gucci loves hip-hop musicians. I know the two statements seem unrelated, but they mean something. Hip-Hop artists feel great flaunting in Gucci clothing because of their visible prints, while Gucci loves the free marketing the artists give them in return.

You will need to design a great logo for your business, distributing it everywhere to become visible to your target market. Moreover, make sure your logo goes with the type of messaging fit for finding target clients.

People should respond in a particular way whenever they use your products and/or services. Your logos and taglines should define your brand. Give your customers a reason for using your products and/or services. Create a feeling toward your logos and taglines.

It is very easy to become viral if your clients are resonating with your company. Your brand may be marketed across the globe for free as clients feel associated with it. A great logo and tagline make marketing and selling easier.

5. Collaborate with other brands

On 10th July 2018, Juventus Football Club acquired the services of one of the greatest football brands. His name was Cristiano Ronaldo, and he was from Real Madrid. Many people thought it was a waste of money to spend $100M Euros on CR7 at thirty-three years old.

On 13th July 2018, Juventus reported they had sold 520,000 jerseys bearing Cristiano Ronaldo's name, worth a total of $60M. These were all sold within 24 hours of signing him. This should teach you something about what CR7 can do, both on and off the pitch. He is not just a goal machine. He is a marketing machine!

Juventus did not buy CR7 only for what he can do on the pitch. They understood Juventus as a club and how he would benefit the club by being associated with Cristiano Ronaldo. This is a guy who had the media following him. Sponsorship companies were trying to lure him.

Pay the price if you can find your CR7 for your business. It can change the way people look at your business whenever you collaborate with other brands. Michael Jordan changed the course of business for Nike with Jordan Air. Starbucks and Spotify was a top collaboration, which made Spotify bigger than before.

6. Live your reputation

Toyota sells more cars than Mercedes-Benz, but the luxury carmaker does not lose sleep over such news. They do not make cars for people who are looking for vehicles just to move from point A to point B. They make cars for people who love status.

This is also true for prostitutes. They are consistent with their brand's message. The ones who target classy clients will never entertain a guy from a lower class. Instead, they stay true to their market and sell to their ideal clients.

You should understand consistency is important to branding. Your brand will not last if you are always changing it, so stay loyal. Everyone in the company should eat, live and sleep your brand.

It doesn't matter when my competition is selling millions of copies of horror fiction because my type of book will only focus on business and personal development. It might take time for people to accept me, but eventually, my name will arise whenever someone is looking for self-help books.

It takes time to build a brand; therefore, you have to stay committed to your brand. Otherwise, you will not have a brand at all. You will easily go from one business to another without establishing a brand, which overall can help your brand in the long run.

7. Protect your brand

They say it takes years to build a name but only seconds to destroy it. It is the same thing with brands. If your brand matters to your business, guard your reputation. Your clients trust your business, so protect it from the attack of their family and friends.

Think about what your actions can do to the trust customers have in your products and/or services. You should do what you assure customers you will do. That is, continue building on your previous successes. Don't ever throw away the reputation of your business.

If you have to hire a public relations person in times of crisis, just do it. Your reputation is your brand, so guard it fiercely.

Chapter Five
DON'T SELL TO THE UNCONVERTIBLE

I have followed marketing trends for a long time. Target marketing is the most commonly used tactic by marketers. It entails focusing on the clients who are interested in your products and/or services.

The first time I analyzed this concept, I remembered how prostitutes focused on guys who understood the art of picking up. They often do not take you seriously if you are new, shy or religious-looking. It's a skill they have mastered, but I am sure they also get it wrong.

Still, the system works. If you are a guy looking for a girl, the best strategy is focusing on a girl who is interested in you. The desire to get your type of girl is cool if you want to caress your ego; however, it's the worst strategy if your focus is execution and results.

The principle of focusing on your ideal clients works in all scenarios. Whether you are looking for employment or trying to close a business deal, I advise you to focus on the companies or business partners that fit your criteria. It wastes time to try so hard until you get what you want because it doesn't yield any results.

As an entrepreneur, your goal is to know the people who need your product. Find ways of reaching out to them. You cannot hope for people to discover you and your products; that is backward thinking.

The world has a population of around 7.8 billion people, but you cannot sell to each person. Therefore, your goal should be to look for people who are eagerly waiting for your solutions. Look for ways of how you can provide solutions to them.

Who are your clients?

This is the first question you should answer about your business. Are your clients young people who are about to go to college? Have they reached retirement age? Are they thinking about investing in retirement benefits? Do your potential clients comprise young ladies who are fashion conscious?

Answering these types of questions makes you understand people. You don't need to waste your time, energy and money on everyone. Sales and marketing can be very expensive when you're not converting the leads into sales. Advertising and branding have never been cheap.

Therefore, it is imperative for a business to put all its time, energy and resources in the place where there will be traction. The business will go through four to five stages before it makes sales. This concept is called "funnel marketing." The easiest way to understand this type of marketing is to look at the funnel you use in the kitchen to pour liquids into containers.

The stages in sales funnels are awareness, consideration, decision-making, and buying.

Awareness — While awareness is primarily at the advertisement stage, its purpose is to let people know of specific products and/or services that you offer. You can do this through social media, TV, radio or print media.

Consideration — This stage gives potential clients the ability to talk about you while comparing you with other businesses. At this stage, your potential clients are very doubtful. They can easily change their mind if they perceive any negative perceptions about your business.

Decision Making — Your client has chosen to buy from your business and, therefore, is just waiting for you to persuade them into purchasing your product and/or service. You need a few selling skills to close the deal.

Buying — This is the stage where every entrepreneur or business owner wants to be. We want to sell and make money as entrepreneurs. You can smile once a client has reached this stage.

Having looked at the funnel stages, you will notice that it is not easy to move a client from start to finish. Some people take days, while others take years. Still, your business cannot wait that long. You need to sell all the time; otherwise, your business will die a natural death.

The goal should be reducing the time frame between awareness and buying. The easiest way to accomplish this is by targeting clients who are in the decision-making process or are ready to buy. Prostitutes are aware of guys that come looking for women. Those types of men want sex immediately and are ready to pay for it.

There is no point in marketing sex to religious men, for they believe it is immoral to have sex with a prostitute. If prostitutes can understand that, then I don't understand why you want to target everyone. Prostitutes understand they only have hours to sell their product; therefore, time is of the essence.

You should know the following as an entrepreneur:

1. Who your potential clients are;
2. What they need;
3. Where they are found;
4. When they buy your kind of products; and,
5. Who they consult when making a buying decision.

Once you have answered these questions, you will find it much easier to sell your products. Your clients will be ready to buy right away. You will not be the kind of business that shoots in the sky and hope the arrow meets a bird.

HOW TO TARGET PEOPLE

Targeting people in marketing and sales will mean intentionally directing your advertising campaigns toward specific groups of people. Usually, these are based on the demographics of clients.

There are two ways you can target potential customers. The first is called demographical targeting, while the other is psychographic targeting. Read below for more in-depth explanations.

Demographical Targeting

This type of targeting is designed for marketing people based on their age, location, gender, income, education, occupation, etc. Let's dive deep into it to explore it further. Then, you will have clarity on how it helps you find the most likely customers to buy your products and/or services.

1. Age

Our tastes for products and/or services tend to change as we grow older. If you look at cars, you will find that Michael could have loved sporty noise cars but changed to luxury cars once he got into his 50s.

Whether it's clothes or real estate, people get attracted to certain products and/or services at different times throughout their lives. A real estate agent listing a family house may get someone in his 20s to buy the house, even though the odds are not in their favor.

2. Location

Your target market will respond differently if the product and/or service require shipping costs. Therefore, offering free shipping for a product and/or service takes the shipping out of the cost.

Should the product require shipping, put any logistics into place before starting to sell the product and/or service. There are countries that may charge some taxes on the arrival of your product and/or service, thereby making it more expensive.

As a business, therefore, you may need to target people from certain locations. This avoids certain logistical implications that might arise because of the location.

The other issue is the product's legality. We all know that firearm sales are not allowed in specific countries, so it will be a waste of money and effort.

3. Gender

Even women can buy clothes for men and vice versa, so targeting men's clothing to women will always be a bad idea for your business.

It is the same with cars and makeup. While most cars are driven by both genders, there are cars that are unpopular by either males or females. Further, makeup is predominately bought by women, while men may also be potential customers.

4. Income Level

There is a motivational post frequently shared on social media, which covers Ferrari's marketing strategy not to place any adverts on TV. They do this because people who can afford to buy their brand don't watch television.

I don't know the whole reason why Ferrari doesn't advertise on TV, but I do know they would never target their adverts to clerks, bus drivers, nurses, teachers, etc.

Why? Income matters. People buy certain products because they have enough money to do so. You might like Rolex watches, but then why would they target you if you cannot afford to buy a Rolex?

5. Education Level

This book is for sale. The plan is to target people who are either business professionals or doing marketing-related work. But still, this is only just a book. Therefore, we will only target people who are able to read. In fact, we will target people who have completed high school and are able to read English.

6. Marital Status

I have written a book called *The Wedding Master Plan*. It focuses on how to get a man to love and marry you; that is, without him being pushy or looking too desperate.

This book is aimed at helping single women understand methods of advertising themselves to men for marriage. The most important thing in the above-mentioned statement above is single women. The book was trying to help single women since it would be dull to target married women.

7. Occupation

Having been a writer for almost five years, I have spent money on things, which others may believe is a waste of money. These include cover design, critique services, line editing, proofreading and formatting my books. These services can only be bought by someone who is involved in writing. In short, this person is a writer by occupation.

Therefore, if your profession is designing book covers or editing books, you would have more customers if you targeted those who have a *writer* or *author* in their social media profile.

8. Ethnic background

We have 73 tribes in Zambia. All the tribes have their own customs and traditions. One thing you cannot remove from a person is the connection to their traditions and customs.

Clever companies associates themselves with certain tribes during particular events. For instance, they will have a poster that says: "Company A is a proud sponsor of the Kuomboka Ceremony."

At a subconscious level, people will make buying decisions based on the connection they have with their tribe. Consequently, if you really wanted to get the Indian business, find a way of targeting people who have Diwali in their social profile.

Psychographic Targeting

This type of targeting focuses on consumer personality traits, values, attitudes, interests, behavior, and lifestyles.

Targeting people based on their psychograph is also another brilliant way of marketing and selling, for these people are most likely to buy your products. In fact, these products and services will easily fit into one of the following areas and make it easier for people to make a buying decision.

1. Personality

Extroverts and introverts don't have the same tastes in clothing, cars, etc., because they buy based on their personality.

Extroverts need to show off, so targeting them with products and/or services, which raise their status, will usually sell. Introverts are reserved and will try to be conservative. This might not always work for everyone; still, most introverts would like products and/or services that are subtle and not so loud.

Personalities include openness, conscientiousness, extroversion, agreeableness, and neuroticism.

Openness — People who are high in openness like an adventure. They are usually open to new products or services. These people are curious and appreciate imagination. If you promise something new and exciting, then you will have a lot of success with open people.

Conscientiousness —Conscientious people are organized and have a strong sense of duty. These people are dependable, disciplined and achievement-focused. Any product and/or service that helps someone look organized and disciplined should be targeted to people with this personality.

Extroversion — Extroverted people are also called social butterflies. They are neighborly, chatty, and love crowds. They tend to love what everyone enjoys. The best way to target them, then, would be to mention that millions of people currently use your product and/or service.

Agreeableness — This measures the extent of a person's warmth and kindness. Prostitutes, for instance, would tell you a story about how they were abused, and you will become a customer based on how truthful you find the story.

Neuroticism — I am sure you have met people who worry too much, thereby having high levels of anxiety. As a result, these people have been customers for most substances like tobacco, security systems, and drugs–all of which promise to ease their nerves.

2. Attitudes

Positive and negative attitudes are relevant, while marketing people to your business.

Positive Attitude — Positive people are optimistic about everything. They believe in seeing the greater good. Positive people will buy your product and/or service based on the fact they believe your business is doing something important within the community.

Negative Attitude — You are wrong if you think you cannot sell to negative people. These people consistently doubt themselves and easily get frustrated. Consequently, you will have to validate all their fears and frustration before you talk about your product and/or service.

3. Values

Christian, Muslim, Buddhist, Indian, European, African, American, Arabic, Asian, Chinese, Zambian and many other values have influenced buying decisions for many people.

People buy based on their Islamic values and beliefs, such as clothing, shoes, and books. Christians and Buddhists buy stuff about Christmas or Diwali based on their beliefs and values.

4. Interests/Hobbies

If you target me with golf products and/or services, I will probably not care. On the contrary, I know someone who plays golf. He has an interest in everything which involves the sport.

Start with caps, shoes, bags, t-shirts and other accessories all about golf. Anyone who targets him with golf products and/or services will do well because his social profiles are all about golf.

5. Lifestyles

Do you know someone who loves clubbing? That's me! It is my frequent visits to nightclubs that helped me learn how to market and sell like a prostitute. I am just kidding.

Clubbing, though, is a lifestyle, which can help you sell more products and/or services. People who like traveling, mountain climbing, singing, public speaking, etc., can be targeted based on these lifestyles.

What I would like you to take from this chapter is that marketing and selling require a lot of effort. It is important for those efforts to be targeted to people who are most likely to buy.

You should never try to sell to everyone because it's a bad move. Put all your efforts and money in marketing to people based on their connections with your products.

Those connections could be age, personality or just a lifestyle. Still, you need to ensure that your products or services are put in front of people who are most likely to buy.

Chapter Six
DEVELOP A SERVICE CULTURE

Robots are taking jobs everywhere. Sometimes, I feel sorry for my unborn grandchildren. It's never going to stop. Technology will wipe out most traditional jobs. At times, this gives me nightmares.

Still, there is hope. It will take time for robots to learn kindness, empathy and obtain a likable personality. Actually, I believe a business with human interaction will be offered at a premium, even if robots take some jobs away. This is all because it will be more costly to be served by a human being.

This is what makes me smile whenever I have nightmares about the effects of technology and our children. Develop a service culture that attracts customers. I don't care how great your products and/or services are. You will soon be out of business if you don't care about your clients.

What does a great service culture look like?

Proactive attitude

So many people complain about work when they have a lot of clients. They complain about boring days when it's not busy due to having too few clients. I, too, have been in these situations.

One day, I asked myself this question: *Am I in control of the day's events, or are the day's events controlling me?* Three-fourths of the time, the events were controlling my day. I was never in charge of how the day should go, and so I reacted to issues almost 95% of the time.

I read a book by Brian Tracy, who focused on time management. It instructed readers on how to plan out the day the night before. Not only did this kind of attitude change my life, but it also improved the way I worked daily. I became more efficient and service-oriented as a result.

I was able to realize what I hadn't done during the day so that I could complete it early the next morning. If I forgot to call a client, for instance, I would put a reminder on a to-do list app on my phone. Then, I would make a call in the morning.

I started planning my days while anticipating issues before they were presented to me. I started challenging myself every single day, trying to work ahead of most of my schedules. It didn't take long before my supervisor and clients started noticing my proactive way of doing things.

Compliments started coming my way; recognition given. Even though the changes were small, they made a big impact on my business. I began planning my day the night before while anticipating the needs of my clients and supervisor. If you can manage this, your clients will appreciate doing business with you. Moreover, they will refer you to their family and friends.

You should know what your clients either want or expect from you, for it is your job to figure this out. Don't wait for any complaints before finding a solution to a client's problem. You should be the first, for example, to realize your website is taking longer to load.

This requires a commitment to continuous improvement. Your clients will be committed to your company once you have mastered this. The wonderful experience of doing business with you will make it harder for them to switch to mediocre service.

Accessibility

I opened my first shop with my wife. It was upstairs and inaccessible to clients because there was neither an elevator nor an escalator. At the time, I did not understand the impact it had on our business. This was until a friend of mine requested I bring her some perfume because she couldn't climb those stairs.

I immediately realized that there so many people like her. These clients would be willing to buy our products, if only it weren't for the stairs. I thought about people in wheelchairs and those who didn't like the idea of sweating because of the stairs.

Your business must be accessible, whether it is online or offline. Let's return to the prostitutes. They go where they can easily be noticed and picked up by men. They don't hide at home and wait for a client. They go to locations where prostitutes are picked; therefore, business is easier that way.

If I am your customer, I don't want to be struggling to find your business. Make it easily available to me so that I don't have to look for it. Do you know why everyone is coming up with an app? It is great for repeat business.

Browsing on Google makes it probable that I may end up on another website. This website may provide products or services similar to your own business. Still, you take me all the way if you create an app for me.

Proper complaint management

You may have great products or services, but you will still encounter a problem at some point. Your client will complain about something that you didn't do right, or maybe your client is not satisfied.

Once I was being trained in a customer service job, and the trainer spoke about how you can turn tragic into magic. You see, not every person you meet is having a good time. People have problems in their families, workplaces, business, religion, cities and/or country.

They have too many problems in their life, which businesses understand. Therefore, they want to help clients turn a bad day into a good one. I want to acknowledge that some clients will genuinely complain about your people, products and/or services. You will then have to address those issues.

Meanwhile, whether you did something right or wrong, you have a responsibility to turn that tragic into magic. Let your client see that you sincerely care. My boss taught me that you need to learn "How to tell a client to go to hell with a smile on your face." He meant you should be courteous and sincere even while you are saying no.

A client should understand that you recognize what they are feeling. Even when you are unable to do something about it, they will be happy. You managed to listen and empathize with them. Always put yourself in your client's shoes whenever handling their complaints.

Solution-focused

The blame game often occurs in many businesses, starting immediately after something goes wrong. People forget what is required when a solution arises. Some people will put all their energy into trying to find the person who dropped the ball while forgetting the client who is suffering due to the same situation.

The world is looking for solutions. Almost everyone on this planet is looking for answers to different types of problems. Therefore, your business should be focused on solving as many problems as possible. Accountability should always be last on your list of priorities.

You should further avoid coming up with products and/or services that suit you instead of your clients. I hope ladies don't misunderstand what am about to say. Do you know why prostitutes do well in their business? They focus on the client.

Nobody pays to make a prostitute enjoy sex. People who go to prostitutes are going because of their own self-interest. Why would someone pay to make another person reach their climax? The opposite is true. You will do better in business once you understand how clients operate from their own selfish interests.

Study your clients so that you come up with products and/or services, which take them to the moon and back. You know what lights the fire and what doesn't. You further know the little details of how to make your clients suckers for your products and/or services, about which your competition does not care or is not well-informed.

Genuine care and building of relationships

In Maslow's hierarchy of needs, love and belonging are at the center of things. Many people can ignore self-actualization, but no one wants to miss out on the sense of connection. We all need people around us. We all want to feel loved and cared for by others.

Still, most business people like to behave like teenage boys, saying, "I love you" to get laid. You can see their ill-will from a distance. Why would you treat your customer like that? It is very insulting to learn that you bought products from a scam business, which doesn't give a damn about their clients.

You should show your clients how much you care. Every business wants to legitimately rob from their clients, but you have to rise above this. Show the world that you are a business with a soul. Be an example of a compassionate business. Your clients will pay more as a result.

Allow yourself to show how you should treat your people and your clients. Set a moral bar for yourself and your people. Your clients should feel proud to be associated with your business.

The ability to listen

You will not be out of business if you start listening to your clients. Clients can help you bring innovation to your business if you are able to listen. Clients will always give you feedback; therefore, it's up to you to do something about it.

I recommend you consider the flow of information to assist you in making business decisions. If your sales lady tells you something three times, then it must be what clients want. You should listen. It might look stupid, but it could be a game-changer.

Deliberately create platforms for clients to give you feedback. Encourage an environment where people are free to speak on innovative ways of improving your business. The guy you hired has the ability to bring in more clients while increasing sales. Start listening.

Living up to your word

It's disappointing when a person or business changes a goal only to suit their selfish needs. Do what you say you will do, and if you have a refund policy–follow it.

Why should you promise guarantees that don't hold water? You should not promise what you cannot deliver because this is dishonest. Moreover, it's an old-fashioned way of doing business. Millennium types of clients will easily sense all your bullshit and find alternatives.

Accountability

I stated above that it is more efficient to focus on solutions instead of looking for someone who has dropped the ball. Having said this, I did not mention people who do not face consequences for dropping the ball.

People should be accountable for their actions. Accountability makes people take responsibility for their actions. It also creates a culture of raising the bar. People who are responsible try, by all means, to give the best they can in every situation.

It eliminates mediocrity and irresponsible behavior. When people are able to understand the responsibility of their actions and realize how they treat clients and each other, only then are both clients and staff empowered. Clients are protected from mediocrity, while staff understand the significance of their daily decisions.

Chapter Seven
MAKE THEM FALL IN LOVE WITH YOUR PRODUCT

Business is all about the customer. Your customers don't care about how fancy your business name is or how beautiful your office looks. What every customer cares about is how your product or service will solve their problem. That's it.

Marks & Spencer makes clothes from factories in Vietnam, Lesotho, and Mongolia. Their clients don't care how these factories look or the reason for producing clothes from these countries. All they care about is another Marks & Spencer product.

Your customers don't have to love the directors of the business or the business itself, but they have to madly fall in love with your products and/or services. Make your products addictive. Create them in such a way that your clients cannot live without them.

People who brag about having an iPhone don't understand why it's almost impossible for them to leave an iPhone for another phone. You lose a lot when you move from iPhone to another smartphone.

They make phones in such a way that you become dependent on them for all your daily activities.

Even your fingers will notice that you are not using an iPhone because of the different features that have been put on the phone itself. Those different features have been put there for a reason. They want you to become so used to an iPhone that it makes you lose the ability to think outside of the phone.

Is it a good thing for iPhone customers? Absolutely yes. iPhone clients don't complain about anything. They love all the features that have been put on their phones. They will line up to buy another iPhone at a premium price every single time.

What about Apple as a company? Are they doing something good for the clients? Yes, and it actually makes them who they are — a trillion-dollar business! They have mastered the art of marketing so well that they can put any premium price onto their products and/or services. Their clients will still buy.

Most iPhone users are madly in love with their phones. They can't easily leave their iPhone for a different phone. In fact, iPhone users will stay with the iPhone for as long as Apple continues to produce more smartphones.

Therefore, following Apple's example, you will need to do the following so that clients fall in love with your products:

Focus on your clients

Marketing and selling are like making love. If you want to make love (not having intercourse — there is a big difference), then you first have to learn what puts your partner in the mood. What tickles them?

People who focus on themselves don't understand lovemaking. You will set the tone, mood, and atmosphere for an unforgettable moment if you are able to focus on your partner. You will know the touchpoints, tease areas and all the little things that make you masterful.

What about business? It's the same principle. You do not understand your business if you do not understand what drives your clients to your office, shop or website. Nobody is going to do that for you. It's your job to know what excites your clients.

I mentioned earlier how prostitutes focus on making their clients have a great experience. They do this without focusing on themselves during those moments. They understand what their clients earnestly desire without uttering a single word.

Package your products irresistible

There is a saying in our language, which mentions how hard it is to sell a cockerel that is wet. A cockerel has exaggerated feathers. It makes them look bigger than they are. But when they are soaked, all that exaggeration goes away, and the feathers return to their actual size.

Great packaging can allow you to charge twice what you already charge. Prostitutes charging $10 look the part, just as prostitutes that charge $1,000 look the part. The way they dress, where they are found, and how they speak all play into their role.

If your packaging is poor, you are going to attract people looking for cheap products. Reflect on the story I mentioned about how Mercedes-Benz positioned itself to attract people who appreciate luxury.

No wonder you do not see a lot of adverts that focus on a SALE for these luxury cars. Sale means cheap. People who buy status don't like buying things because of discounts. Therefore, it is important to understand your target market and package accordingly.

Identify your clients' needs

The world is full of problems. Internationally, people are complaining about the lack of certain necessities for their well-being. The worst-case scenario is when an entrepreneur joins the multitudes of complaining people.

"Whenever I see people complaining, I see opportunities." — Jack Ma (Founder of Alibaba).

The basic reason prostitutes sell sex to people who do not love them is that they provide solutions whenever those people are in desperate need of sex. Imagine finding water in the desert. People would beg you to sell your water to them.

That's how you sell. You should think about people's needs in your product's design, distribution and sales process. You can never wish or hope for more sales. You should complete enough market research to specifically know which products and/or services people want. Actually, you should find the type of products and/or services that people DESPERATELY NEED.

Get into the mind of your potential client, try to understand what s/he is looking to buy. You should know what triggers them, as well as what makes them give away their hard-earned money. You should know the deeper psychology of your buyers. It is as simple as that.

Sell feelings

Within the selling and marketing world, 'people make buying decisions emotionally and justify them logically.' Therefore, your duty is to understand your customers' feelings. This should give you an idea that "what you say and how you say it" really matters.

There is a big difference between "This car has a 12 horsepower engine, giving it the ability to drive 360kms/hour" and "Imagine how your girlfriend would feel if you picked her up in a 12 horsepower car which drove 360/hour." Learn how to sell feelings.

"The nighttime city lights of this house will give you a great feeling."

"This type of suit will make you appear like a boss."

"Taste the feeling." — Coca-Cola.

All the statements above portray certain feelings toward prospects. Whether someone wants to buy a house, car or drink, there is a feeling attached to it. The feeling can be significance, happiness in a family, or quenching of thirst or love.

Whenever your client feels a certain way about your product–and those feelings are pleasant or agreeable–you will not need to pitch too much before you close. Your client will see himself or herself experiencing those feelings way before they get your product. Feelings will easily make your clients make a buying decision.

Offer solutions

If you have ever been affected by a computer virus, you probably don't question why you need to pay for antivirus software. You know the exact pain you went through, not to mention the effects of lost information due to clearing the virus.

Many people and companies buy antivirus programs to protect their systems from trojans and malware. People would not have any use for antivirus if these hostile applications were not there.

This also applies to website hosting. If you have a website and the deadline to pay the hosting fee is due, then you will do whatever it takes to keep your website running. This is because website hosting is a solution to your business. It is part of what makes your business run.

You should further design products and/or services that are solutions for your customers. Come up with products that solve a certain problem. Prostitutes know how some people can get desperate when they want sex. They know how important sex can be.

And so, they decided to sell it at a premium. They know the other alternatives require marriage, a relationship or some form of bonding. This is what made sex a premium product. I see it going to the New York Stock Exchange (NYSE) one of these days.

There is a solution you can provide in whatever industry you pursue. Look for problems, complaints, and encumbrances. Marketing and selling will become easier once you sort out issues with your product.

Focus on quality and excellence

Product development plays a big role in the marketing and selling of your products and/or services. This is why it's important to focus on solving problems for your clients, even before you launch your product and/or service.

Notwithstanding, the quality of your product and/or service is key. While developing a service culture, I emphasized the importance of giving clients a wow experience. These wow experiences can only come if products and/or services were designed to provide those experiences.

They say it takes six months to make a Rolls-Royce and 13 hours to make a Toyota. This is not much of a time frame comparison; all the same, I am stressing that you need to do more for your clients if you want them to do business with you.

I am not trying to praise prostitutes in this book; still, I have to mention some marriages experience unpleasant sexual experiences. In turn, this makes them seek out better experiences somewhere else. This is a lesson for businesses as well as couples.

Always give the best you can and don't settle. Continuously improve on your skills, making every encounter exciting for your clients. Make your clients look forward to doing business with you. You can't afford to offer boring and irrelevant products and/or services.

Your clients will start cheating on you before they divorce you, ultimately leaving you for a business, which cares about quality and excellence.

User-friendly — don't complicate your products and/or services

There is something I love about Facebook. Facebook designers are gurus. You don't need to be educated to use Facebook, for even the most uneducated people know how to use it. I hope you don't think they created it like that for no reason.

Facebook has an amazing 2.4 billion subscribers as I write this book. Do you know why it possible to have such numbers? Simplicity. Don't create products and/or services that are difficult to use by people of any educational level.

Create your products and/or services in such a way that a grandmother can both use and show her friends how to go about it. Facebook has managed to attract those numbers because their website and app is very simple to use.

You don't have to guess how to use the platform. It just asks you to post what is on your mind. Who can fail to do that? They have included symbols and buttons, helping even those who can't read to use it.

Create manuals where you find it necessary. These are useful if your product and/or service are difficult to install in its current state. Moreover, consider hiring people who can help your clients with the installation. You will have to pay more for it, but it's worth it if you have not yet created a user-friendly product and/or service.

Remember my story about the stairs and how it affected my business? Don't make the same mistake. Make your office, store or website easily accessible by almost everyone. Have a child's brain as you create your products and/or services.

Simplify as much as possible, creating a great user experience for products and/or services by those who decide to do business with you.

Chapter Eight
OBSERVE THE MARKET AND LEARN NEW TRENDS

You should be able to remember floppy disks and burning CDs if you are in your 30s. I remember infrared as a way of transferring information between phones. The good old days were great in many ways.

People would boast about how invested they were with software for which I can't remember the name. People asserted how good they were at driving manual cars, and some of them would even refuse to buy an automatic car.

People will not be driving cars within the next 30 years, but rather cars will be driving people. I can see mundane work being done by robots while people are stuck with the old ways of doing things. As a result, they are being told to leave their jobs.

If you think only employed people will be affected, then you need to reconsider your position. Some businesses will be replaced by other types of businesses. I remember a guy in my community, who was making a lot of money by selling scratch cards for airtime. He stuck in there till after he lost all his money.

Let's talk a bit about the best marketers of all time — prostitutes. They know all the cities, roads, night clubs, and hotels where there is business. Likewise, they know the locations that don't add value to their business. No wonder some clubs hire some prostitutes to pose, for they are in fear of losing business.

The other things you will see prostitutes doing very well are their attire, as well as the type of music making the charts. They try to get themselves the most appealing and fashionable clothing on the market so that they are able to attract attention.

If you are in business, you need to question if your products and/or services will be relevant five to ten years from today. It is likely that your business may be digitized or replaced completely.

The following are some things you need to do right now. These will help you remain relevant, assuring you are on the top of your game:

Invest in digital business intelligence

We are living in one of the best moments of our lives with the potential capabilities of the internet. So many tools can show you consumer behavior and buying habits. Google Trends, for example, is one of the digital tools you can use to learn about what is trending within your industry.

Follow your industry influencers and publications

Some strategic moves you can make right away are in the papers. Every industry has influencers who share their wisdom in articles and newspapers.

You should subscribe to all the authoritative influencers and publications if you are a purebred marketer or salesperson. These provide daily insights on marketing and sales. All the new trends in this field are available at your fingertips.

Listen to what your clients say

The above-mentioned advice is relevant to staying prominent in your industry. Your customers may offer a solution to you and offer to pay for it. They could be looking for a solution, sharing it with you through a complaint.

As a marketer and salesperson, you can easily find out what your customers want from review platforms. Pay attention to what your customers are suggesting and implement these ideas into your business.

Review websites like Yelp are goldmines for people who want to know customers' needs. Instead of just looking at what your customers say as complaints, look at them as solutions.

Pay attention to what your competition is doing

In Zambia, there is one company I have always followed. I am interested in how they market their products. They are not my competition, but their marketing is brilliant.

Trade Kings is the company's name. This company has grown so big, and all thanks go to their marketing team. Most of their marketing campaigns are captivating and interesting.

If you cannot come up with marketing tactics but you compete with Trade Kings, then it is okay for you to watch and understand their marketing strategies concepts.

Once you understand that people easily connect with products and/services that relate to their loved ones, you can find a way of connecting it to a child. This is opposed to Trade Kings' method, in which the company uses someone's mother.

Allow a bottom-up flow of ideas — your employees are smarter than you think

If you have a child who was born between 2006 and 2019, I can correctly guess you wonder how your own children seem to be smarter than you. And they are!

It is surprising if you agree that your children seem to be smarter, but you still refuse to accept the new breed of your workforce. This comprises a generation that knows more than you.

And let me tell you why.

The old folks believed in learning from classes and experiences, while the new kids believe that they can Google anything. They can find the same answers you got after sitting in boring classes for years.

Create a business environment where people feel their opinions are valued. Don't be a leader who has all the ideas. Ask the right questions, paying attention to what people are saying.

If possible, get a book and a pen. Jot down every idea worth testing. We are living in a fast-paced world. Therefore, you cannot tell where a brilliant idea will come. It's up to you to come up with an open-door policy for your business.

If you are a leader, it's time you started getting advice from the young. Be like a prostitute for once! Those guys leverage their networks of young pros.

They ask for fashion and the new trends for their businesses, becoming unstoppable when it is combined with experience.

Surround yourself with smart people

Birds of a feather flock together. You will be dumb if you spend a lot of time with dumb people. I can't reemphasize this point for you to understand the influence close people have on your life.

Don't be scared to look stupid in front of smart people. It's better to look stupid around smart people than looking smart around dumb people. Getting comfortable with the wrong people can be the reason why you are struggling in both life and business right now.

The only way you will attract smart people in your life is by cutting out dumb people. Let them go. Introduce your dumb friends to other dumb people. Like minds attract, so they will be happy together.

As soon as you get rid of dumb people, you will see personalities that will challenge you. Most importantly, these will bring value to your life. The difference will be visible. You will grow as a person, and your business will flourish.

Ask the right questions

I don't know whether you know that this book is a how-to book. A lot of people will insist it will not work while never asking how it will work.

Every question you ask has an answer. The answer can either bring solutions or show you more problems. After discovering that, I realized I was getting the right answers after asking the right questions.

You should never ask why something will not work, but rather remember that it will work. You should not ask for challenges, but instead, solutions. You should never ask why people are not performing but how they can start performing.

Ask the right questions.

Anticipate and embrace change

There was a new type of business in Zambia, becoming popular in the early 2000s. It was offered in booths, and it started as a result of the cell phone's introduction.

In those times, very few people could afford to buy a phone; therefore, people had to go to the booths and make their phone calls or send text messages. It sounds crazy, but it was very real in those days.

Couples in distant places used to utilize this service very well. You could see them inconveniencing others due to taking longer on those paid cell phones.

And you know what entrepreneurs did? They bought more phones! This allowed couples to make their calls easily without being disturbed by others. Relationships became better, and so business grew for the booths' owners.

It didn't take long, though, before phones became affordable for ordinary people. The telecoms wanted more subscribers. The only way for them to increase subscribers was to make it possible for everyone to have a phone in their hand.

You probably know what happened. Calling and texting through cell phones, which was originally offered by booths, started to struggle. All the people who stayed in that business till the end lost money. That kind of business was simply dead.

The clever ones moved on to scratch cards. Since everyone had phones, it was now time to sell airtime scratch cards. The first people who got into that business made a lot of money. Some of them were even given wholesale opportunities by telecoms.

By 2009, smartphones had become popular. Everyone wanted to have a smartphone. Still, smartphones came with their own challenges. Do you know what the first entrepreneurs did? They started getting smartphone covers, screen protectors, batteries and chargers for these phones. As a result, they made a killing out of this business.

Between 2010 and 2017, there was an increase in mobile money transfers. Before that, the transfer of money was mostly done by banks and a few other institutions, like the post office and Western Union.

Telecoms saw an opportunity. They started working on their own mobile money systems, and it soon became a game-changer. There was an opportunity for guys in the booths. These were people who see an opportunity for what it is–opportunity.

They also made money before the booths were flooded on the market. Business is tough, but technology is brutal. You can go under overnight due to the introduction of a competitor's app.

The booth story is an example of what technology can do to your business. You can either use it to your advantage or get annihilated.

If you are in business right now, you should anticipate and embrace innovation. I usually laugh at guys who brag about going for a business trip in UAE or China in 2019.

Why should I travel to China to select tires or jeans when I can go elsewhere and build a relationship with a supplier? This new type of business requires new thinking. The art of doing business is the same as it always has been; going astray will get you in trouble.

Innovate and continuously improve.

Chapter Nine

CLOSE AGGRESSIVELY AND UNAPOLOGETICALLY

"Put that coffee down! Coffee is for closers only," said Alec Baldwin in the movie *Glengarry Glenn Ross*. This is a 1992 American drama, which looked at two days of four real estate salesmen. These salesmen needed to close deals, or they got fired.

Anyone can pitch a new product, but closing the sale is for people with brass balls. Being a salesperson is hard. People will give you all types of excuses for not buying from you. If you are a true closer, you will find a way to push your products and/or services to the world until someone buys your product and/or service.

All in all, it's not easy.

Six challenges in closing:

1. People will lie, saying that they don't have time or money.
2. You can't force people to buy your products and/or services.
3. The more you push as a salesperson, the more suspicious you become to your customers and the guys in compliance.
4. You believed the stupid story of a bad economy.
5. You lack enough motivation to sell your products and/or services.
6. You are too modest and shy.

Do you know what it takes to stand in the streets, waiting for someone to pick you up for sex? What about being in the night club, drinking water while waiting for someone to ask you to join their table? Can you handle that?

It takes guts and strong willpower to do what prostitutes do. Some people say they are possessed or maybe on drugs. I think a salesperson needs a little of both to close deals. People will criticize you, but still, you shouldn't give a damn about what anyone thinks.

You should never be that type of salesperson who easily believes what customers say about money or time as they are objecting to your products and/or services. People always have enough money and time, but you are not at the top of their priorities. It is your duty to make them put your product and/or service on top.

There are so many rules against salespeople in trying to protect consumers from pseudo sellers. There is a thin line between being a great salesperson and a fraud. People will always see you as the latter, so your job is to stay on the right side of that line.

In good and bad economies, there are people who make money selling products and/or services. The story you get in the news about people being broke has always been there. It should not stop you from selling.

You should also look at what motivates you to sell your products and/or services. I don't care whether it's money, passion or self-actualization. You should focus on what drives you to sell. Only then will you sell more because you'll have something that gets you out of bed.

Meanwhile, I am aware of being too modest. If you asked people who knew me as I was growing up, they would tell you about a modest or timid Edwin Ngwane. I was taught to be reserved.

After years of self-awareness, however, I realized it was not worth it. I know so many people who think my younger self was too pompous and loud. At the same time, I don't care because I don't live my life for anyone. I am unapologetic. Life favors those who take two seats while others are fighting for a chair.

Being modest and shy might be great attributes when looking to apply for a position at your church, although these are not recommended when you want to market or sell your products and/or services. Leave your modesty and shyness at the door.

SALES CLOSING STEPS

Know your client

I have consistently repeated this statement because it works. In the banking world, we provide solutions based on the needs of the client. Who is your client? Do you know what s/he wants?

Once you identify your potential client, it becomes easier to target them. You can advertise specific products to them that suit their needs. This pertains to client value proposition (CVP), which is an element of relevancy.

In simple terms, CVP refers to a clear statement that addresses three things: relevancy, value, and differentiation. By already knowing your client, you will be relevant in your business and your brand. This gives more value to your clients, especially since you will treat them differently based on their specific needs.

Spend time with them

Do you know where your clients are found? Social media is no longer just for kids. It's time you changed your perspective.

What about finding clients online? Did you know that Tesla-one of the biggest car makers-closed its retail outlets in 2019? They will sell their cars online directly from their plants. Some of you have smaller businesses and may think online business is for small boys and girls.

Do your research. People are spending more time on their smartphones and computers. As a salesperson, you should know how to use social media and Google to your advantage. Therefore, you will find more clients and close more sales.

Salespeople of the past had to follow their prospects to their homes to close a deal. But guess what? Now you can follow your prospect into the toilet. You will get your client's attention faster and close the deal sooner.

Discover their fantasy

Do you know why you don't sell products and/or services? It is your inability to discover what turns on your customer. Every person has his or her weak spot. Listening to your customer will allow you to learn about all the things they care about. It could be a dog, car, children, spouse, parents or job.

If someone talks about their mother while you are trying to convince him or her to buy a house, change the conversation. Start talking about the nice features of the house, asking them what their mother would like about that house.

If you think I am crazy, then pay attention to university adverts. These focus on how you can easily get promoted with their MBA. You will discover that after getting the MBA, it was great to get the MBA but not for the reasons with which you were presented.

The reason prostitutes perform better in their marketing and selling is that they have discovered people have sexual fantasies. These fantasies are real to their clients. Prostitutes arouse those fantasies by making them more visible while their customers beg to get hold of their products.

Address their risks and fears

No one in their right senses would go to a prostitute without a second thought. What if this person is a serial killer? What if they drug me and take all my money? What if I contract sexually transmitted diseases? What will people say when they see me with a prostitute?

These questions will always be there. It is further true for your clients. What if your product and/or service don't work as you promised? What if you are a scam? Will you just take away their money? What if you sell products and/or services that can end up bringing criminal charges to their doorstep?

Your clients are human beings, and no human being enjoys looking stupid. Remember, we all like to have a good standing in society. Even though you are a junkie when you are alone, you always try to look normal whenever you are with others.

It is a normal human reaction. The question to you is this: How do you address your customers' fears? Prostitutes would tell their customers to pretend as if they never met, even when I meet with a partner. That's a great assurance.

They would similarly tell their customers that they have their own house; therefore, their clients don't have to be seen leaving a hotel with a prostitute. When they go about doing rounds, assurance of protection will also be provided. What about you? What assurances have you given your customers who intend to buy your products and/or services?

This book has an assurance in case you did not see it. It states- "WRITER'S GUARANTEE:-Please contact us if this book neither helps you nor teaches you something new. We will not hesitate to refund you."

Do you have what it does? It makes you feel comfortable making a purchase. You risked losing money on a bogus book with a useless title, such as *How to Market And Sell Like A Prostitute* as soon as you picked this book.

There is a reason why products and/or services have manuals and guarantees. It is not just a selling gimmick but also a statement that defines belief in your product. Who would put a refund policy on a product? You would lose money if you did that.

This would put you in a position that makes you look like your products and/or services are better than your competition. It shows your commitment to satisfying your clients better than your competition.

Forget the features and talk about how they will feel

I remember being at the night club counter. I heard someone whispering in my ears while touching my waist. She whispered, "I will make you feel like no one has ever made you feel." I didn't go there for anything like that, but I was taken at that moment.

Salespeople enjoy talking about the features of a product and/or service. This product and/or service is good because of A, B or C. Some people also like to talk about their companies.

Talking about your company draws in your customer. Speak to them about your company's background, its goals and what the company has accomplished. Tell the client of past clients and how you have helped them. It helps you to build credibility overall, but it does not help your customer.

Some salespeople take it to a good level. They speak about the benefits of their products and/or services to the customer. However, it does not persuade your customer to buy.

You need to learn how to speak to your clients about your products and/or services in regard to how it affects their emotions. Feelings sell more products and/or services.

Talking about your customer's emotions while using your products and/or services is very powerful and can improve your sales. It will make your customers beg you. People make their decisions emotionally, so you must back them up logically.

As you relate their feelings to your products and/or services, it forces clients to desire your brand. In short, you will put your clients in the mood to buy right away.

Don't offer more than three options

If you go to any of your favorite fast food restaurants, you will notice that three offers are always given—small, medium and large. You might think it is just one of those things, but I can assure you that it is all marketing and selling.

Average is a common mentality for most people. As human beings, we don't like small things , and we also don't like to go beyond the standard. Therefore, we like to choose something in the middle.

It has been studied that people make their buying decisions easily if they are presented with fewer options. If you present more than three options, then your customer will be confused and postpone the transaction.

This type of behavior becomes an opportunity for a business. You have to create products and/or services that bring clients to your business while increasing the profits of your company.

If you look closely, the medium option is expensive when you compare it with the other two options. And that's where you'll find your steak if you do it that way.

Another option is to bundle your products and/or services. Bundling a slow-selling product with a good profit margin will sell fast but with little profit.

You can do that even in situations where you are introducing a new product and/or service. Bundle the already well-known product with a complementary product that is new on the market. It will not take long before people love your new product.

Don't counter customer objections–use them

Imagine you finished pitching your products and/or services. Your customer says, "Your product is too expensive. I don't have money." I am sure your first response will be to defend your product.

Managing objections is part of the closing process. If you fail to address clients' objections, then you will not earn the client's money. The mistake salespeople make is that they try to counter customer objections.

Let me share something with you. Countering a customer's objection is insulting and very undermining. This is a sign you have not learnt a lesson that a client with money is wiser than you. Meanwhile, you still want to get his or her business.

Instead of trying to counter his or her objections, practice how to use them. You should not focus on why your product and/or service is too expensive, but rather illustrate to your client that you understand their reasoning and emotions. Then, ask clients what they would consider offering you in order to make the deal more fairly priced.

You can benefit more by looking at the product and/or service from the customer's angle. It will give you an opportunity to probe them with questions, finding out what matters to them. Remember the CVP. The relevancy of your products depends on so many things.

At the same time, you can only understand the criteria if you are able to listen to your client. You must be able to see the whole picture. You might learn more about their decision-making or what they have gone through in the past.

A client who objects to your offers is right. Your job is to mention that you understand their fears. It is okay for them to feel unsure before experiencing a new product. Talk about how another customer felt the same way, but then they ended up becoming your loyal customer.

Essentially, you must validate your customers' fears, using their fears to see the whole picture from their perspective. This makes you look genuine and understand their point of view. It also helps you create products and/or services that suit your clients' needs.

Talk about what you can do–not what you have done

The worst type of conversation between a prostitute and a potential client would include references to past transactions with previous customers. I don't think it would help to close a sale.

The future is exciting. The past is usually boring. You may make a mistake by mentioning something that your previous customer liked, but as it turns out, it is hated by the current one.

To further this point, no one will truly believe you. It is for this reason that you don't write your own testimonials. Instead, your customers write or speak testimonials in their own words.

Therefore, it is important to excite your clients with what you can do instead of what you have done in the past. Saying you used to do something has never been an interesting part of any conversation.

Ask for it–don't be shy

Customers get confused whenever making a buying decision. Actually, confusion arises if they are buying a product and/or service from a new company. Therefore, it is our job as salespeople to guide them in the right direction.

This is called a 'call to action' in marketing. It has to be clear and precise. If you are giving out a trial product and/or service, say so. The most important thing is your client knows what they must do next.

You cannot afford to have your client guessing about the next course of action. S/he should either be buying or not buying; therefore, make it clear and precise about what your customer is supposed to do.

There is a fictional story shared in bars about a Catholic Father and a nun, both of whom were driving from one village to another. It is told that a nun sat in a compromised way, where the left side of her thigh became visible to the Father.

The Father gazed at those beautiful thighs and got confused. He was consistently on and off the thighs as he drove through the bushes. The nun pretended not to have seen this heated Father, but still, she was interested.

They were both playing "holier than thou." Neither of the two wanted to make the first move but instead waited for the other to make the first move. *What if she says no?* What will he think of me? Both these questions were lingering in their minds.

They both decided to play it safe. The Father tried whistling as he was panting, while the nun could only cough. He tried changing gears with the hope of touching the thigh; though, he always missed.

The nun decided to unbutton her blouse, revealing a bit of her breast, which confused the Father. As he was sweating and driving, the nun decided to give him what he wanted. Though she said it in such a way that he would understand. She said, "Mathew 7:7."

She immediately knew the Father did not dare to look to the side where the nun was seated. He was too embarrassed. At this point, the nun was almost undressed. She repeated the verse, but the Father could not hear anything.

He was thinking about what the nun would think about him after that incident. At that moment, he felt so bad that he couldn't say another word to the nun after she spoke, "Mathew 7:7."

The nun was frustrated and concerned with what the Father will think of her. She hastily got out of the car and left as soon as they arrived. After the nun left, the Father decided to read what was on Mathew 7:7.

And guess what he found? "Ask, and you shall be given."

This happens all the time in marketing and selling. You can advertise and position your products and/or services while hoping they get enough attention. Still, you will not close the sale if you fail to ask your clients to buy. Just imagine if the Father knew that verse.

Don't be shy. Reach out your hand shamelessly until you get what you want. Who knows? Maybe the person you are afraid to ask has always wanted to give you what you are seeking.

Ask, and it shall be given to you.

Follow up

Let's go back to the story of the Father and the nun. What would have happened if the Father went back to the nun, telling her he now understands Mathew 7:7? Remember, this verse was given by a willing giver. She could have been desperate at that moment.

If you are a salesperson, but you do not follow up with your prospective customers, then you don't know the importance of your sales game. If your client tells you that s/he is not ready today, ask when they are going to be ready.

You need persistence. Toughen your mental muscles if you are someone who gives up easily. You shouldn't feel anything when a customer turns down your offers. It's just part of the sales process!

As a salesperson, I would tell you that my biggest move for selling was "referrals and follow-ups." Whenever I got a client, I asked for five referrals from each of them. Then, I followed through with those referrals.

I created a network of clients from just one client, thus making sure I followed up wherever necessary. You should try this tactic. It works like magic. However, it requires you to make a lot of follow-ups before you can close the sale.

There will be no money without any closed sales. Therefore, it is important that you are aggressive and unapologetic about closing sales. This is where you will find your bread and butter.

Chapter Ten
SPEAK TO THEIR MIND AND SOUL

Words are powerful. People might call you slick or talkative, but you first have to be a master at communication. Speaking to clients will get you attention overall.

You should develop charisma that allows you to influence people with your words. People will criticize you or hate you, but I will tell you how to handle these kinds of people.

In the absence of marketing or selling, you will find it difficult to sell anything. Products like this book make a lot of noise. You will see it on social media, TV, radio as people endorse it.

There is a high probability that if you criticized this book in the first place, then you have become curious. You have finally bought it. I hate to see Coca-Cola adverts on TV. They make a lot of noise while I wait for news headlines.

In spite of that, I will admit to drinking Coke, even when I know that it is not good for my health. I also want you to pay attention to the voices used for advertising. Wow! The voice is deep and smooth for guys, while ladies tend to speak beautiful and sweet.

There is power in speaking if you want to market and sell; however, you have to speak to influence. You need to speak tactfully to get people's attention. You must know how to speak to their mind and soul. Get to their mind and control their spirit.

Share stories

On 30th November 2019, I got home from work after a tiresome day, only to find a priority mail envelope waiting for me. My wife mentioned that it was from the US.

I started wondering what was in that envelope. It was small, and it didn't look like items I usually buy on Amazon. "What could it be?" I asked myself.

I have to be truthful with you. I admire being an American. I actually plan to live there once my plans work out. My destination will probably be Austin, Texas while Charlotte, North Carolina is my second choice.

In my spare time, I sometimes look for condos for sale that are located in either Austin or Charlotte. Redfin.com is my go-to website as I fantasize about buying a condo in America.

Returning to my main story, I asked my wife to open it for me. I was so interested in learning what was inside that white envelope from the United States. Upon entering the bedroom, however, I heard my wife shout: "Honey, it's a check from Amazon!"

"What? A check? How much?" I inquired. These were my questions as I ran back to the sitting room. Before she could answer, I was holding a $250 check in my hands.

It was from Amazon's Kindle sales for my book, *The Wedding Master Plan*. I couldn't believe it. I never thought it would come to pass, but it finally did. It was beautiful to finally get something out of my hard work. I felt good.

Let me tell you something. One of the above stories might not be true. I may not have gotten a check from Amazon, or I might never plan to live in the US. Still, you followed those stories very well.

We naturally love stories as people. "Once upon a time" has never stopped captivating people's hearts. Watch TV adverts with the mindset of learning how to market and sell. Only then will you will see a lot of adverts that tell stories about what can interest you.

You should consider telling stories about your products and/or services. Tell stories about your successes and failures. Tell people how you got started, as well as everything you went through before becoming a success.

The people who connect with your stories will always be attracted to your products and/or services. Some of your stories will not work, but most of them will make an impact.

Flatter the clients

If you give a lady a compliment, there is a chance she will like you. Men, too, love compliments. No, let me put this from the right perspective: we all love compliments.

The best way to make people fall for you is by making them feel better all the time. Do this flattery, especially if it is genuine. Human beings like to feel like gods. They almost want to be worshiped.

It is that yearning for flattery that you can use to attract people to fall for your products and/or services. Don't talk about how good they may be. Talk about how amazing customers will look or feel while using your products/services.

Instead of creating marketing campaigns that focus on your business, try coming up with ideas for campaigns that speak directly to your customer. "Ladies, I use product ABC just like you." This has been used to persuade prospects for a long time. Create one for your own business.

Find a way of singing praises for your customers; worship them. Talk about how wonderful they are and all the things they do. Talk about them in all the wonderful aspects you can ever imagine. They will love you as they pour their money into your business.

Smile consistently

It's very difficult to keep a sad face when you meet someone who puts a warm smile on your face. A smile is infectious. It attracts other smiles. Science has also proved that as soon as you smile, you tend to make your mind and heart believe that you are happy.

In short, you can invoke happiness by sharing your smile. You can change someone's day by putting a smile on your face. You can make your customers happy by being the kind of salesperson who smiles consistently.

Wear that smile. While it is free, the results can be worth millions. A great salesperson is someone whose customers feel obligated to do business with someone based on how s/he makes them feel. It is beautiful to make people happy while making money in the process.

Look into their eyes

The ability to make good eye contact is one of the best social skills you can bring to the table while marketing and selling. It is a skill every salesperson should polish for his or her own selfish reason.

Numerous studies have shown that people with higher levels of eye contact are perceived as being:

- Warm and personable;
- Attractive and likable;
- Qualified, skilled, competent and valuable;

- Trustworthy, honest and sincere; and
- Confident and emotionally stable.

Increased eye contact does not only make you appealing to others. It improves the quality of interaction with others. Eye contact portrays a sense of intimacy with people around you, leaving them feeling more positive about your interaction.

Making greater eye contact with customers can increase the quality of all your face-to-face interactions. Nowhere else in your life will you be seen as attractive, confident and more trustworthy than eye contact.

Being able to look people in the eye while holding their gaze can help you in networking, landing a new job, getting laid, or intimidating your enemies. Most importantly, it can improve how you pitch your products and/or services.

Eye contact can also allow you to read your potential customer's thoughts. You will be able to tell whether your customer is paying attention, lying or uninterested.

Be confidently warm

You may have heard about alpha males. These guys walk and talk slowly. While sitting, they spread their legs and extend their other arm into the next chair. They are annoyingly confident.

Have you ever doubted your confidence? I guess you have done that more than once if you partake in introspection. It does not feel right when you can't walk tall.

The worst part is when you learn that nobody is attracted to a timid person. Confidence is very attractable. It has the ability to heat up space, making both the person and place warm.

Consider a lady's confidence as she tells a guy she likes him. This is called reverse engineering. Most men tend to feel great, especially those with a strong character. Even ladies love men with confidence.

Some people are born with a lot of confidence. Joy - my daughter, was born with it. The rest of us have to build it. I encourage you to fake it until you make it. Even your clients want someone who is very confident about himself or herself.

You can't sell anything if you are unable to walk tall. If you are waiting for someone, take up enough space with relaxed shoulders. Greet people with a firm business handshake. Learn to speak slowly and clearly.

The most important part of feeling confident, however, is by loving yourself. You should know that you were wonderfully and fearfully made. It is important you start feeling as if you just killed a lion.

Use humor effectively

I love comedy. It brings euphoria and removes resistance. If you can make your customer laugh, you will definitely close the sale. In the business world, people tend to be too serious. Most people are sad.

Do you know why most people are stressed? They don't find enough things to laugh at while in business. People with a sense of humor report less stress and anxiety than those with a low sense of humor despite experiencing the same problems in their business.

Business is tough, and so a little humor can re-energize you when you are on your last nerve. Using humor in organizations is associated with improving morale among workers.

As a marketer and salesperson, you should know how to use humor in your messaging to your customers. At the same time, don't overuse it. I cannot personally count the number of adverts I love on TV, all because they make me laugh.

Whenever I go shopping, laughter drives me to the same product and/or service. Anything which makes you laugh will definitely make you happy. Products presented in this way make you happy; therefore, they are easy to buy.

Use humor in your advertisement. It also increases the chances of people accepting new ideas and products. You will also get people to pay attention to what you are selling. It's not easy for your customers to reject a product and/or service while they are laughing.

Contextualize the message

If your target market is a 50-year-old, your messaging should be suitable for your target group. It would surprise me if 50 years old were lining up for this book's signing session.

This book is for entrepreneurs and business owners who want solutions that are kind of radical. I did not write this book to impress book critics or those who think they know it all. I wrote this book for the few who want to find gold.

The book title and tagline are way out of line for most people, but I don't care. Do you know why? The people who find my book outrageous are not my target market. I can even recommend Zig Ziglar's books for those kinds of people.

We live in a world that makes us target people based on their likes. This type of marketing makes it easier to contextualize our message in marketing. If someone likes football, for example, an advert that talks about tennis won't work for them.

You need to return from where we started. Know your potential clients and then target them based on their needs. You can't be using the same message to market or sell to everyone, for you will lose if you do that.

Whatever communication you make with your clients, make it personal to them. In this digital age, we have tools that can contextualize your message. If you want my business, you have to learn how to speak in the way I like.

You should watch how prostitutes do it. If the guy s/he is spending time with is a Chelsea supporter, s/he will become a Chelsea die-hard immediately. You will be surprised to meet that person the next day, wearing a Real Madrid FC jersey.

Speak to the heart

Passion wins votes and gets people laid. Do you know why? People who speak with passion tend to speak to our hearts. We tend to fall in love with them in those moments.

Whenever you hear about someone charismatic or persuasive, you will see a person who speaks with emotions and addresses the little things that matter to your heart. If you are married or don't want to buy something, run away from such kind of people.

As you advertise, try to describe your products and/or services in such a way that clients feel something. Prostitutes use this technique all the time. You can easily fall for their juice if you are not careful.

Don't be opinionated–general is good

Opinions have always created wars and divided people. I wonder why people are so opinionated. Avoid opinions if you are a salesperson. Stop telling clients about your religion or way of life.

The biggest problem with opinions is the conflict they create. Why would you go about telling people about what they should do or how they should say things? It is none of your business!

Be general about things, especially when you are talking to another opinionated person. I am not saying you should not believe in something or your business, but instead, do not share opinions, which are irrelevant to your products and/or services.

Avoid talking about things that have nothing to do with your business. Politics, religion, race, tribe, gender, nationality, etc., are not things you should include in your marketing or selling conversations.

Whether you are playing golf or having a beer with your client, be very general about your discussions. If possible, agree with everyone. Listen to them while saying nothing about your beliefs and/or opinions.

Consistency is the key–Repetition

Standing true to your message is another key aspect of making people fall for your products and/or services. You should never be inconsistent in your messaging. Being true to your taglines, inform your customers of any re-branding that involves your products and/or services.

Be consistent if you support a cause, such as keeping the world green and clean. If you claim that your products and/or services help people in their client acquisition, remain in that lane for as long as your business is in operation.

Chapter Eleven
RIDE AND GRIND LIKE NO OTHER

What puzzles me about life is this: so many people would like to be successful, but most of them are comfortable with the status quo. They do exactly what their grandfather did, hoping that something different will happen.

You will not be successful with the same old mentality of your grandfather without working hard. You should first get rid of the old ways before you can embrace success.

Marketing and selling do not end with the customer buying the product and/or service. You need to ensure they use your product and enjoy the experience. In essence, you cannot afford to have your product become junk in your customers' home or office.

Ensure your product, service and sales experience is exceptional. Repeat business is the long-term strategy for selling. I have sold more products through referrals than I have through cold sales.

If you want to create a successful company, you should plan your marketing and selling for the long-term. There is no point in making huge sales in a few years, only to close your business a year later.

Therefore, your marketing and selling will thrive if your customer likes and buys your product and/or service. We explored this in the previous chapters.

However, as a business focused on the long run, we need our customer to enjoy and promote our products and/or services to their family and friends. We need to transform our customers into salespeople.

The only way we can do that is by putting in the work and building our company. This process requires thinking more about the customer while also being committed to giving a satisfying experience from your products and/or services.

Start with the end in mind

The first aspect of your business is creating a vision. What do you want to achieve? Where do you want to be in 10 years? How are you going to do it? What resources do you need to get where you want to be? Do you have a mental picture of what you want to create?

You will not achieve your desires without a vision. You need to address all the issues. This includes how your customers will like your products and/or services, as well as what will make them promote the products and/or services.

There should be a proper plan detailing all the activities. This, in turn, will help to execute your vision. You will fail to impress your customers without a proper plan in place.

Give more than you take

You have probably been in a situation where the other person cares more about themselves while thinking less about you. How did you feel? Imagine a situation where there isn't reciprocation between you and others.

It doesn't feel right to be the only one receiving, nor does it feel right when you are the only one giving. As I say this, some poor people might say they don't have anything to give.

In business, though, you should give more than you get. This strategy makes your customers happy while annoying your competitors. Most businesses like to rip off customers. If you are doing the right thing, you are bound to be in business for a long time.

Haven't you wondered why restaurants give playing spaces to kids without charging you for it? Think about businesses that provide free installation after selling you a product and/or service that requires you to pay for installation.

All the businesses that have this understood the principle of giving more than they receive. No one likes to be ripped off. Your customers know that you are a business; therefore, they will not contribute to you like a charity.

You have to demonstrate that you care about them. Give more to them than what you get, and likewise, your competitors will wonder how you did it.

Be flexible and do what your client wants

If a client wants vanilla cake, would you give them a chocolate cake? The answer is probably no. In essence, you need to respect your customers' wishes in order to succeed in business.

Don't force your customers to buy what you want. If you do not have the product and/or service they want, then you should advise them where they can find an alternative.

This will make your customers like you more, and it shows your customer that you value them more than the money they give you.

Stay on top

I once wrote an article on LinkedIn that stated: "Success is like a white shirt–good to get but hard to maintain." It is the same with marketing and selling. Ask any salesperson about the difficulties of consistently exceeding sales targets. It's tough!

In spite of those challenges, you need to find a way to stay on top. Once you fail to be on top of things, your customers will not be satisfied. In fact, they will start seeking out alternatives sooner than later.

Things typically go wrong as you try to make customers happy. You will definitely encounter a few problems, but you have to stay committed until your customer is satisfied.

All this information and strategies help you stay connected with your customers. Ask them what they enjoy and what keeps them coming back. Ask your customers to provide feedback on areas that you could improve.

Listening to clients and implementing around 50% of their suggestions will give you the opportunity to enhance the overall experience between you and your customers. It will be more beneficial than it was previously.

Your customers will start to feel as if your company is their own. As a result, your customer will be proud of their association with your company. As long as you continue to improve your business while always giving them a satisfying experience, your brand and sales will increase.

Show that you know your stuff

Recently, upon moving into a new house, our landlord completed some renovations and enhancements before we moved inside. She hired an expert to assist with the renovations.

However, when the man first arrived at our home, he came unprepared for the job. He didn't have any tools (not even a measuring tape). There was neither a renovation plan nor any solutions. I don't know much about carpentry or home decoration, but I soon began losing patience.

We had this guy for about a week, and nothing changed. He actually did more damage to the house than how he found it. And he had excuses for everything. It seemed as if he never had enough time-all the time.

Another week passed before we requested the replacement of this guy with someone else. The second person came with the landlord, just as the first had. It was only five minutes into the job, and I was certain this guy would do a great job. He had no carpentry tools the first day he came; however, that did not stop me from being persuaded by this guy.

Upon coming into the house, he inquired about the issues we'd requested for rectification or enhancement. We showed him what needed to be completed; then, he pulled out his smartphone to take photos of all the areas that needed attention.

He told us he would not be available for the next two days, and we were okay with it. Sunday-the day he promised us he'd return-he was at our place at 9:00 a.m. as we had agreed. He brought all the necessary tools with him.

His tools included a ladder, paint remover, small tubes and a few other things, which (as I layman) I didn't find necessary. When he started working on our home's renovations, I started noticing how everything he had carried was being used on his project.

This guy was amazing. He took everything into consideration. There would be painting to do, for instance, after he was finished with renovations. If there were a small drop, then he would have to remove it from the tiles.

I didn't understand why this was important until my wife spoke about it. I realized he had done a lot of work similar to this, but women tend to complain about such stuff. And so, he doesn't leave it to chance because of his knowledge and experience.

My question to you is this: *What do your customers think about your products and/or services?* Look and act the part, for instance, if you are helping people with event management.

You cannot afford to have customers doubt your abilities or your business. Consequently, you will always struggle with marketing and selling your products and/or services.

You should reach expertise within your business, thereby encouraging people to make you their go-to company. They will return to your store for particular products and/or services. Don't be an amateur for your entire life.

Be passionate and committed to the ride

My last thoughts on this topic: *How long can you go?* We all know untalented players score at some point in their lives, although this doesn't occur often.

Didier Drogba, Cristiano Ronaldo, and Lionel Messi are legends for good reason. These players consistently delivered when it most mattered.

These guys dug deep, finding a goal when nearly everyone on their team was about to give up. You would see these guys scoring winning goals in the 88th, 89th, 90th minute and even scoring the last kick of the game.

The other question: *How do they do what they do?* The answer is very simple. These guys are passionate about their sport. They love what they do, and they are committed to giving the best every time.

Anyone can do it when they are in the mood, although doing it well requires some passion and commitment. Only a few can do it. Only legends can do that.

A lot of businesses say no as their default answer. They feel as if saying no is doing the right thing. What about going the extra mile?

It is better to get out of business than to stay in a business that is not exciting to you. Anyone that does exciting work will tell you they enjoy it, even if the work is tough.

Learn to do the light extra things that your customers want. You don't need to break the bank to go the extra mile. The little things are nimble and human, but still, these matter to all of us.

If you can touch people in their soft spots while making it a priority to go the extra mile, it is impossible to fail in marketing and selling to customers. Actually, your customers will do it all for you.

Chapter Twelve
BREAK THE RULES AND BE READY TO FIGHT

Upon meeting people for the first time, you realize everyone has specific beliefs about everything. Unconsciously, you are always required to adapt to the surroundings. Therefore, you can easily relate to others.

Still, it becomes difficult when people want things that are different to your own agenda. What are you supposed to do? Are you going to surrender to their needs and/or wants? Will you go against everything to achieve your goal?

Imagine a situation where you are told everything you want to do is unacceptable. The issue is not about the illegality of what you want to do. Instead, it is unacceptable to other people.

We have too many rules in life, so it is difficult for a person who wants to achieve something great. It's nearly impossible to follow some of these rules; therefore, it is fine for you to break the rules. If nobody has given you this permission, then you have it now.

I am not talking about breaking the law but instead regulations. Laws are usually enforced by governments and meant for people to follow. They are specifically written, designed so precisely that they can be interpreted in courts of law. Legal action will be taken against you when you break the law.

Rules, on the other hand, are set up by people based on their own beliefs. You will find most laws are the same internationally, while rules can be different from one home to another.

Thus, it is possible someone close to you (such as your mother or father) could create a rule, which might do more damage to you. This is based on the fact that your parents do not know any better.

You might also have a boss at work whose rules might make the whole team dysfunctional based on his lack of leadership. S/he will, therefore, create BS rules, which overall, hurts the performance of the team.

Even if you know better, you will not allow your boss to do that to your team. After all, you would break the rules. Furthermore, you break the rules if you realize your parents are creating rules that can help further your goals.

Rules also exist in marketing and selling. People that don't understand anything about business will laze around, telling you all the BS rules. They claim these rules hurt your performance as a marketer and/or salesperson.

It is my responsibility, therefore, to start rewiring your brains right now. Understand what BS is in conjunction with what is good. For instance, you will shout if you are sitting in a quiet room, and you want everyone's attention.

By shouting, however, you might imply breaking the rules. If you feel like your boss is only using you (and rewarding you), then you will tell him so. But guess what? He might get offended.

Therefore, it important to learn how to smell bullshit wrapped in a rule. You have to break free from it upon smelling it. Let's start with breaking the rules found in your society.

Attract attention

If you are employed, you will hear gossip about a guy who is an attention-seeker. People will speak badly about this person, alleging how they got promoted due to their attention-seeking behavior.

My question to such people has been this: *Why don't you do the same thing?* They usually say it is immoral to get promoted like that. Hypocrites! That's what I call such people.

In *The Wedding Master Plan*, I wrote about how a beautiful lady would struggle to find a husband. That is, of course, if she does not seek out men's attention. How will she get married if men don't see her?

There are so many people who think that seeking attention is a bad thing. It is not. Some people are just afraid of getting enough attention. They do not know what to do with it once they have it.

Attention is what you need if you are a marketer and/or salesperson. Donald Trump once said that there is no such thing as a bad reputation. People who are known are people who get what they want.

Many things are possible if you can get enough attention. Donald Trump managed to become President of the United States. This is because he always understood what getting attention could do for himself and his business.

Use a bit of braggadocio

Humility is a good thing for rich people. Sometimes, I am bewildered hearing poor people speak about humility. How can you talk about being humble when you are in a humbling situation?

The only people who can legitimately claim to be humble are people with power or money. Try to raise your profile a little if you don't have either of these. You cannot afford to try to be humble. Are you trying to become a beggar?

People should always see you like someone on a mission. You should never look like a loser. I have been poor most of my life, but I have always behaved like a rich guy.

I don't buy stuff to look rich. Instead, my mindset is that of a winner. My spirit cannot be broken, and my faith has always been unwavering. I see a king in me. I have big dreams, and I have never been shy to share them.

I remember sharing my dreams with friends and colleagues, even though most of them laughed at me. I was living in the ghetto at that time, and the mental picture I was portraying was way too big for them to believe.

They say that God is there, though they should see me now.

Proclaim big things about your life. Don't shy away from sharing your big dreams. Don't be afraid of planning to buy a Mercedes-Benz. Don't be afraid of setting higher targets as you start out in marketing and/or selling.

Prepare your mind, making yourself believe you are bigger than what most people think. Treat yourself like a king. It might look like you are proud to some people, but who cares?

Life is all how you make it. It is about how you feel about yourself. It doesn't matter if you have not been meeting your goals. You have to start behaving like a winner today.

Put your eyes on the money

There is common trash talk about why money is unimportant. What worries me about this stupid talk is this: it is the very rich and the very poor who talk like that.

Rich people have no audacity to talk about the unimportance of money they still hold on to, while poor people can't talk about money that they haven't earned.

A salesperson or marketer who believes that money is not important will not go that far. You should do charity work. The only problem with that kind of work is that you will still be asking for money.

Money is of the utmost importance to those involved in the marketing and selling of products and/or services. Money is the oil that runs businesses; therefore, you cannot afford to lose your perspective on it.

Put your eyes on the money. Learn everything about how you can make more of it. Don't forget sales, whether you are selling for passion or as a hobby.

Any person who doesn't pay attention to the money is not good for business. This book is all about getting your products and/or services to your customers so that they can earn money. Marketing and selling involve money, even if you are doing it for charity. Therefore, it is imperative for you to understand money's importance. Money is a good thing. It is not the root of all evil, but instead, it will solve 99% of your problems.

Get it, and you will thank me later.

Screw everyone, if possible

Another rule you should debunk: never screw people close to you. The world is all about you; therefore, nobody will exist if you die right now. People exist because you are alive.

Chances are that different people will cross paths with you as you try to push your products and/or services to the market. Those people might be your parents, church friends, colleagues, friends or spouse. They may not agree with you because of your beliefs.

Instead, they will remind you of what you stand for as a tribe, church, family, relationship, or organization. People who are close to you will stick all the BS rules on your face just so they can stop you.

All you have to do is to screw them all. You should never feel guilty for doing what you believe is right. If someone close to you does not believe in what you want to achieve, then part company.

You will later realize that certain people are not good for you. They might be nice people and may care for you; on the contrary, you still have to cut them loose for your own selfish reasons.

If you have to decide between failing with people close to you and succeeding without them, always choose the latter. They will actually thank you for having made the right decision.

Perfection is a weakness

I know so many people who believe in living an impeccable life. I usually wish them luck in their journey. This book is not perfect, but you'll realize this if you have read it this far.

The Few Who Find Gold was the first book I wrote and published. I will tell you it is one of the best books I have written. This is not based on how well the book was written but instead based on the fact that I managed to write it.

I had feedback from "supposedly better authors" who were still writing a great book. They taught me about structure and pronouns. The good thing about it was that I listened to their advice while they were still polishing their debut book.

I sometimes read through my manuscript, laughing at all the mistakes I made in my first book. I am amused by the incorrect grammar and formatting found within that book. I once got tempted to perfect it, but instead, I told myself to leave it as it was.

The time will come when that book selsl based on my passion and not the perfection of grammar. Most importantly, I will always thank myself for having made that decision.

You should realize that perfection is the reason why you may not achieve your dreams. You are always waiting for the perfect time, opportunity, mindset, prospect, business, etc.

Perfectionism has paralyzed so many dreams and ambitions. Every time you want to launch something, a voice is telling you not to do it. You feel there is more to be done whenever you want to launch your product and/or service.

When is the perfect time? What do you consider perfect? Who decides what is perfect and what is not? Are you procrastinating or still trying to be perfect? Are you aware that most things you consider perfect today were launched before they were perfect?

Let me tell you something if you are Mr. or Ms. Perfect. It will challenge the way you think. While you are waiting for your product and/or service to be perfect, another person will launch it.

This person will be called a legend. The only thing you will be remembered for is the same old boring story you will be sharing. You had a much better idea first, but no one will believe you.

Stop being a nice guy

There is a friend of mine who used to say he couldn't buy lunch for a lady unless there was something between them. According to him, there is a certain level of abuse directed at good guys.

Funnily enough, it reminded me of the time when I was 19. I liked a certain girl at school, so I would do all the nice things for her. I hoped she would consider me her boyfriend.

One day, as I was escorting her to her home, we met a guy who she introduced as a boyfriend. When the guy inquired about me, she said, "Edwin is just a nice guy, a brother to me."

This might look so basic to you, but it happens in organizations, relationships, and businesses. You will find an employee who is overlooked, receiving only a pat on their back.

There are relationships where a partner's sacrifice and commitment tend to look like BAU to the other person. People have a tendency to abuse good people, and I'm not sure why this is.

If you are a nice person, you've probably been abused by the people you helped. It's possible they even made you believe that it is your responsibility to help them. Bad people have no limits on how nasty they can be.

Therefore, it is important to know when to be nice and when to be nasty. Stop acting nice to anyone that gets your referred customers as a complementary business. After all, they don't return the favor.

If excuses become typical of your company, look for someone to fire. Set an example for people to stop taking you for granted. I have done this to people who have taken advantage of me.

We live in a world where people thrive on taking advantage of good people. It is wrong for good people to allow it. Even good people should be able to say no. Don't allow people to use you for being a nice guy.

Avoid being like everyone

Whether you like it or not, people want you to be like them. They want you to believe what they believe while behaving in the exact same ways. That is an ideal situation as a marketer or a salesperson.

People like to buy products and/or services from people and companies who are similar to them. No wonder you will see a lot of mimicry around marketing and selling. However, it is just not feasible to be liked by everyone.

Therefore, forget the idea of being like anyone in order to be liked. Break the rule of fitting in. Most people are average, so you will be liked as you join the masses.

Your alternative is to take your own path and follow it.

Embrace failure

I was recently watching Anthony Joshua being beaten by Andy Ruiz Jr. for the Unified IBF, WBA and WBO boxing championships. The first thing that came to my mind was how Joshua would respond to this:

They asked him about the defeat, and he responded that it was just a minor setback. Then his promoter said that Joshua needed to reclaim the championship in the next rematch. Otherwise, he would be finished.

I did not agree with his promoter. Joshua might have lost a boxing match and even the rematch; still, it is not the end of his career. Most people try to put the heaviness of failure on others instead of lifting it up.

Every person should understand that one day, we all will fall. Your face will touch the ground; you will feel powerless. This does not just happen in boxing but in all walks of life. Defeat is inevitable.

There is also an opportunity to rise again, though, every time you fall. Tiger Woods has done it, as has Michael Phelps and Joshua. You should never feel like it is not okay to fail. It is okay.

What matters most is how many times you rise back up instead of how many times you fall. People will mock you and make you feel like a loser but remember to embrace failure as a minor setback.

Motivate your critics

My wife once saw me having a troll with people from all over the world on social media. It was about Donald Trump being one of the best presidents. Some people called me names and insulted me.

She was surprised that in all those moments, I seemed to enjoy the experience. She told me she wouldn't want to be in my position at any time.

You should realize that not everyone will agree with you. I am a full-time supporter of Donald Trump, and I am not ashamed to say so.

He is a genius. But I also understand and respect certain groups of people who will not agree with me.

What makes Donald Trump a genius is that he knows how to infuriate his critics. They motivate him by criticizing him. You need to re-learn marketing and selling if you think Donald Trump does most things without thinking.

Every move Donald Trump makes is about getting the media's attention. He doesn't care whether they talk badly about him or support him, just as long as they are talking about him. He knows that there is no such thing as bad publicity.

Check out the Kardashians if you disagree. These are personalities who have surrounded themselves with controversy. They actually fuel it. They want you to talk about it, and in essence, they motivate people to talk more about them.

As a result, they get more attention the more people talk about them. It doesn't matter whether you say good or bad things; they will still get attention. If you know what attention does to a business or brand, then you also understand why they do what they do. It is a case of polarity.

Pray for misfortune on your competitors

I know your mother told you to pray for others. But what kind of prayers do you pray? Do you pray your friends should prosper? Do you pray your competitor should get that contract? Do you pray your competitors should have everything going well?

I know you are lying to everyone when you say you pray that your enemies will be well. The truth is, you and I both wish ourselves well while praying for some misfortune for our competitors. You might not agree, and I understand. Once you cut the crap, however, we both know where you stand.

Let your haters hang

The challenge you will face in marketing and selling is that you will have haters. These people will see something bad in everything you do. They probably feel you are not good enough to earn their money.

Some people who will hate your products and/or services are very close to you. We have a fallacy of believing people close to us cannot have feelings of hatred. Wake up!

Ask politicians. Their sons, daughters, wives, husbands, etc., reveal their secrets to the media. There is always that disgruntled person who can do you harm.

But should that bother you? Absolutely not. Let your haters hang. The good thing is that evil people usually drink their own poison. They use their own rope to hang. Don't waste your energy on unimportant things and/or people.

Spend your efforts on trying to push your products and/or services to your customers. Leave all the critics and haters to hang themselves. If possible, watch as they hang or drink their poison.

If a fight comes to you, fight!

This may sound like a contradiction, but it is not. I told you to let your haters or critics hang, but what if they bring the fight to you? Are you going to leave them alone? Is that not going to give them more ammunition to hurt your business?

Imagine a competitor paying crooked journalists to post useless stories about your products and/or services. Think about a corrupt politician pushing for the closure of your business, solely based on the fact that s/he has been paid by your competitors. Are you going to just leave your business?

No! You will have to fight. This may include another PR counter-attack, sponsoring a politician to beat the crooked politician, or taking legal action where there may be sufficient evidence. You have to fight where you haven't any choice other than fighting back.

Apologize for nothing

Running a business is not easy. You will definitely cross paths with people at certain points in your business. Particular people may not like your aggression or pushy behavior, but it's a wise sales strategy.

The worst thing you can do as a marketer or salesperson is apologizing for everything. How many times are you going to apologize? People will blame you for discontinuing a product. Are you going to apologize for that too?

What about firing an incompetent worker or closing a business where people will lose jobs? Are you going to stand in front of the cameras and make a public apology? No! As long as there is no ill-intention in your actions, you should apologize for anything.

If you can-create new rules

The final part of breaking the rules is creating new ones. If you are old enough, you will remember that selfies were not something most people appreciated. It was seen as a type of narcissistic behavior.

After a few years, however, even the people who were against selfies are posting them on their social media profiles. This happens in business marketing and selling situations. There are so many rules attributed to marketing and selling, but one thing that is primarily important is supply and demand.

Supply becomes less effective when you get higher quantities of it through a specific marketing or selling technique. I laugh upon seeing people still painting all types of products in their shops in this era.

Any marketer or salesperson understands the power of moving with time. You cannot afford to remain in the past while marketing and selling. A proper salesperson tries and tests many things in order to get their customers' attention.

Some tactics will not work, although some definitely do. The most important part is your willingness to change. Create new rules about marketing and selling until you find rules that will work for you.

Chapter Thirteen
BUILD RELATIONSHIPS

Building and managing client relationships are at the heart of any business. The cost of acquiring clients is way too high for any business to fail, so it's vital to keep the ones you already have. Time and effort are essential in acquiring clients, yet few businesses spend time to nurture already established relationships with customers.

People don't understand that repeat business is cheaper and profitable for your business. You will easily get more money from an existing client while it will take time to optimize a new client. The key to making money overall is by winning and keeping customers.

The only way you will keep clients is by building a relationship with them. However, building and managing client relationships take a lot of hard work over a lengthy period. This is why failed businesses fail. Some have even tried to automate relationships with clients, but still, this has failed terribly.

How do you manage a relationship with a client?

Engaging in client relationships is the same way you manage a relationship with any other person, whether it is your partner, parent, child, etc. Any relationship will require an effort to make it work. You must put in the time, effort and commitment. And there must be a mutual goal of giving each other whatever the other person wants.

You should always remember a client is a human being. Stop looking at clients as numbers. They will leave your business as a result, going instead to businesses that will treat them like people. In consequence, you will remain with numbers, and the clients will still just be numbered.

MANAGING A RELATIONSHIP

Imagine working so hard to become rich while you yearn for all the wealth. How would being independently wealthy affect you? It would feel nice for me because I am on that journey, and I will become successful as a result.

It is not easy to become rich. Most successful people have worked hard to reach their successes. They failed so many times, fighting a few battles before they finally got the sweet honey pot.

It is the same with business. Consider how hard it is to get one customer to trust your products and/or services. It is not easy. You will go through objections and rejections before finally getting your loyal customers.

Once customers have trusted you with their money, how are you going to treat them? The cost of acquiring customers is much higher than the cost of nurturing their business relationship.

Think about it. If you have a loyal customer who usually visits your business, they will spend money with you. But if you are trying too hard to acquire the customer, they may not spend a cent on your business.

Therefore, building and managing customer relationships are critical. Relationship management is the key to a business' survival. This is the best move if you want to be in business for a long time.

Steps to managing a relationship:

Under Promise and Over Deliver

The worst business mistake you can make is not keeping promises. Do not promise customers something if you fail to follow through on it. This, in itself, is very disrespectful and insulting to your customers. I have been in those situations. I understand how embarrassing it feels to tell your customer you have failed to do what you guaranteed.

The remedy is simple–don't over-promise anything. Tell your customer you will do it to the best of your skills while putting a disclaimer on it.

Another way is to be honest in your communication. If you are truthful about what you can and cannot do, it is easier to satisfy your customers' desires.

Know what matters to them

A business with many customers can neither assume all their customers like the same things, nor do the customers enjoy being treated the same way. Doing these will only cause problems in managing customer relationships.

Long-term customers have a reason for doing so. Have you asked them? It is important to know why the customer returns to your business; therefore, you can repeat this strategy with future customers. Moreover, is important to ask why the customer leaves because this is room for improvement.

It's all about paying attention to what customers say. We already covered feedback in the previous chapters, discussing why it matters that we understand our customers better. So, we can now continue to give them exceptional service.

Call the customer by the name s/he prefers. Some of your customers might not be interested in your calls, but still, they appreciate visits to their offices. Most importantly, you must understand what each customer likes about your business.

Show that you genuinely care

Let me tell you a story.

One day, I was walking across Cairo Road in Lusaka when a guy began asking for transport money. He narrated a story to me, saying that he came from Kabwe Town. The person he came to see in Lusaka was not responding to his calls, so he decided to go back.

The problem was that he had already used some of his transport money. He only needed around K50 (USD5) to make up his full transport fare. I was touched by his story, but at that time, I did not have money.

Therefore, I started asking questions so that we could find an alternative. I asked if he could come with me, so he could ask a colleague for K50. Or, he could consider going in the evening with a friend who was returning to Ndola.

Once I said I did not have money, however, all my other suggestions fell onto deaf ears. This guy stopped listening to me. He actually looked as if I was wasting his time with these suggestions.

This guy's story got to me without a doubt, and I felt I needed to help him. But the more I tried, the more I started to feel as if he was only looking for money. He was not looking for a solution to going back to Kabwe. He was only seeking money.

The moment I realized this guy's position, I left for my business, only to find him at the same spot at 5 p.m. He was still looking for transport to Kabwe. My point in this real-life situation is this: every customer with whom you do business knows when you are genuine and when you are not.

This guy did not care about anything else but money. He wanted to be helped, but he had no regard for the people who were trying to help. It is possible it was a scam, but it was very disappointing. He didn't seem to care about anybody (or anything else) but money.

You should always remember that customers are human beings. If you want to understand people, you should first understand yourself. You should do some introspection about what you like and dislike. Consider how you are treated by the companies from which you buy stuff yourself.

You have probably experienced marketers or salespeople who seem to be more interested in getting your money rather than forming a relationship with you. Whenever you talk about money, they seem excited but lose their enthusiasm as soon as you ask for a solution.

Your customers are not fools. They will smell your BS almost all the time. You will only lose if you are a business owner or entrepreneur who wants to scam people out of their hard-earned money.

Be trustworthy

Can you be trusted? Are you the type of business that keeps its promises? Do you honor guarantees? These are small things, which can sour a business's relationship with a customer.

There was a time I was using a Viva Video application. I got it from Google Play for creating videos for my social media profiles. They indicated that once you pay for VIP, you will have access to all the VIP features with one click.

I purchased the VIP features for USD13.99, clicking the upgrade feature. However, I was surprised I was still accessing the same basic features after paying my premium subscription. And so, I read their FAQ. It requested that VIP subscribers uninstall and re-install the application if the challenges continued.

After the new install, I still didn't have any VIP features. They further indicated VIP subscribers would have access to the support team for resolving such issues. After contacting them, I still have yet to hear anything back.

After realizing I was getting nowhere with this application, I canceled my subscription and looked for another application that provided the service I needed. The amount was too small to ask for a refund, but I have no kind words when it comes to speaking about the Viva Video app.

It is dishonest to claim that someone will have VIP features once they pay while then failing to do so afterward. It is fraudulent to tell people to pay for VIP customer support and fail to give it to them.

All these kinds of experiences make customers realize you care more about their money instead of providing a service. I know some businesses might survive with these fraudulent schemes, but if you want to make customers your brand ambassadors, then you have to be trustworthy.

Don't let pettiness screw you

My previous example of the Viva Video experience might also be a situation where I was just being petty as a client. It is possible. As a business, you will have situations, which might drag you down.

Relationship management is not easy. Customers can go out of line sometimes. They might unnerve you. Some customers might complain about petty stuff, which does not make sense.

You need to stand calm and firm in these situations. If you have a situation that is almost pulling you off the lack, learn to stay calm and collected. Those moments with customers will always be there.

It is your job as a relationship manager to ensure pettiness does not ruin your customer relationship. Move with a cool head at all times while avoid being overtaken by emotions in all customer interactions.

Focus on convenience

Clients are looking for convenience. They are willing to pay premium prices for products and/or services, which provide this convenience. If your products and/or services are not designed in a way that's convenient for your customer, then it's time to redesign your brand.

Ask yourself questions like this: *How can we help our customers' not waste time while doing business with us? How simple is our platform for customers' usage? What can we do to make our customers enjoy the experience while doing business with us?*

These questions will help you find solutions. But the best way to accomplish this is by asking your customers. Conduct a survey, asking your customers what they find more convenient about doing business with you.

A convenient platform is very difficult to leave. Your customers will not leave easily if they are satisfied with what they receive from your business. Convenience will help you keep your relationship with your customer.

Innovation must be at the center of your business if you truly intend to provide convenience to customers. There are so many tools that have increased customer and business interactions.

Therefore, you must decide which tools you will need for your business. Choose tools that will benefit your customers. Once you make a decision on those two things, you will see the results of providing customers convenience.

Communicate often. Don't be forgotten.

Most customers, if asked why they switched to another company, will say your business was too quiet to remember. In short, they forgot about you.

I believe businesses should digitize, but they should still keep a human element in relationship management. Communication is an integral part of any relationship. Without this, relationships soon die.

Whether you are a leader or looking for love, you lose the game if you fail to effectively communicate with others. A study claimed it is better to over-communicate than to have less communication.

The consequences of not communicating with your customers are too grave to take for granted. Set up a deliberate communication program in your business so that communication with your customers is measurable.

You cannot afford to be forgotten by your customers.

Create a freemium structure

Free, standard and premium are common pricing methods used by most service businesses. This type of pricing is called freemium. It means that you can start with a free service, upgrade it to the standard package and get the premium offer if you want more features.

This pricing method helps you with three things:

1. It helps you acquire customers who still doubt your products and/or services through a free offering. It gives you a chance to ask customers to try your products and/or services for free. You end up having more clients try out your products while others are moving toward paying offers. These advanced packages have more features.
2. It builds a relationship with your customers as they move through all the pricing structures. It means they have appreciated the lower versions of your products and/or services. Therefore, they can trust you by paying for the premium offers.
3. It can further increase your revenue. The customers you get through free offers will eventually start paying for some of your premium offers. This produces leads through the capturing and management platform. After you have acquired the customer through the free offers, you will be able to upsell the premium offers. After all, they are already enjoying your basic features.

This pricing strategy helps you keep customers for as long as your business exists. If your customer hasn't any money, they can still use your services without considering your competition's alternatives.

Customers can easily downgrade or upgrade from free to premium, depending on their needs and financial capacity. This puts you at an advantage since you will keep your customers in all types of situations.

Customer confidentiality

Why would someone do business with you if you can't protect their confidentiality? We are living in a digital world. As a result, you will definitely have access to information about your clients. Henceforth, you have the responsibility to protect their privacy and confidentiality.

Personal data is essential to many decisions made about us. Information about us can affect whether we can get a loan, a license or a job. It can affect our personal and professional reputation. There are so many decisions that can affect how we continue to live our lives, all the result of information made public about us.

We may do a lot of things, which, if judged from afar, may seem old or embarrassing. Our clients may start to wonder why they did business with us at all because of how we handled their information.

Business is a game of trust. People trust you before they do business with you. They know that you will protect their interest while keeping their information private at all times. As a business, you have an obligation to keep information about your clients confidential.

Some clients will have access to your products and/or services. These people would not like to be associated with your type of business in public. Politicians and religious leaders would not appreciate being mentioned in an advertisement, which portrayed them as VIP members of a strip joint.

Customers whose confidentiality was breached could sue your business, costing you and time and money in the court system instead of making money. The people who choose to do business with you have different reasons for accessing your products and/or services.

The following are some reasons why your clients wouldn't want their business dealings with you to be made public:

1. Conflict of Interest

Clients who buy your products may work for a competitor company. Imagine a Coca-Cola CEO who loves Pepsi. It would be inappropriate and stupid for Pepsi to make an advertisement that shows the CEO of Coca-Cola drinking Pepsi.

2. Respect for individuals

Privacy is about respecting other people. Someone may have a personal or reasonable desire to keep their business interests with you private. So it is, therefore, disrespectful to ignore their wishes without a legal reason.

3. Reputation Management

Your clients could be public officials who receive a lot of scrutiny and condemnation about everything they do. They could be against a certain drug publicly because of political will but personally accessing that drug from you.

4. Legal Battles

Some businesses, such as the health industry, will have access to clients' private health problems. These clients would not like that information to be made public. If you are careless, you would be sued, and it might not end well for your business.

5. Trust

The last thing you want from your clients and/or potential clients is broken trust. You run the risk of soon being out of business if your clients cannot trust you to keep their information private. No one will trust you enough to do business with you.

If you want to market and sell like a prostitute, you should be able to do business with someone. Act like you do not know them publicly if that is what they want. You are not allowed to talk about anything in regard to your clients if they have not given consent.

Keeping your clients' information private will protect you from having to explain or justify yourself to your clients since you did not protect their confidentiality. You do not want to put your clients in an embarrassing situation. It could make them explain themselves to their spouses, children, relatives or the public at large for doing business with you.

There are so many reasons why people might choose not to have their business dealings with you made public. It's not up to you to decide what to reveal or not. You can only make your clients' information public if you are legally bound or given consent to do so by your client.

Chapter Fourteen
LEVERAGE ON THE NEW CROP OF PROS

There is a common saying that says, "Whatever goes up, must come down." This is true for most things. It's easy to get to the top, but it's hard to stay there. Everyone is fighting to take your spot. You should be able to fight and defend your territory as much as you can.

However, you have to understand that it's not easy to accomplish this only with your wisdom and genius. You need to realize that as you grow older, you begin to lose perspective about certain aspects of life. It is the young ones who can come to your aid.

When prostitutes grow up, they find it difficult to attract as many customers as they did when they were young. They begin to use their connections to introduce high-paying individuals to the great-looking and vibrant young ones who join them in this business.

They almost always work like PIMPs (people who connect prostitutes with clients as a middle person). This works for normal businesses like yours. If you are a lawyer, the time will come when you will be asked to join a case. Usually, this is a case where you did not source information, but rather some lawyers are based on your experience and expertise.

If you are in construction, this is the time when you tend to get contracts. You begin using the capacity of young construction companies by subcontracting projects. You might look like you are throwing away cash, but you may have decided to become smarter later in your life.

When you have seen it all and what remains is wisdom and connections, then you need to begin saving your energy for important things. If you can, hire young ones to start running the business. Then, you can spend your time with your grandchildren.

Let the young ones take over from where you left the business. Empower them with wisdom and expertise. This will be your time to leave a legacy for which people are going to remember you. In the case of prostitutes, some people may not see much value. Still, the whole picture of how they sell a product shouldn't be sold, for it is genius.

Therefore, it is important to know when to step away from the dance floor. Clap for the dancers who you coached and mentored. The few strategies below will help you find, nurture, coach and inspire new pros who will take over for you.

The good part about what I will share with you is that you will leave a legacy for a lifetime.

Look for the hungry ones

When I started working as a direct sales representative in 2008, I had no idea I would end up in the banking world. Selling is not easy. Most of my friends gave up and resigned, while others got fired for failing to meet their targets.

But I didn't see any other way. I just couldn't give up. I received a lot of scorn from people telling me about how "lucky" I am for being promoted to management. I laugh about it because I know what those people lack in their pursuit of success.

Hunger for success has helped me to reach this far. One strategy I have always used to position myself for the next job is by going above me to help people succeed. The more recognition I get, the more I reach out to help others.

People who have managed me have been very successful. Some of them got promoted because they had me on their team. I am a valuable resource, always determined to give the best at all times.

I will tell you that the people who pick me are more brilliant than I am. They take advantage of my own hunger for success for their own benefit. Are they bad people? No, they are not. They just know how to pick the best.

If you are managing a team of marketing or salespeople, you have to go for the best. The best does not mean having a résumé or college degree. You have to find what drives this person. A person who has his own ambition will always perform at a higher level.

The people who have coached Lionel Messi claim to be good coaches. Still, it is Lionel Messi's desire to win that has made some of those coaches look like they are so good.

Pick winners for your team if you want to win. Look for the people who are hungry. These are the people who will succeed, even without your close supervision.

Coach and motivate them

As soon as you find young, hungry lions and lionesses, teach them how to tear prey apart. Show them where to hunt and who to hunt.

It is your job to inspire these hungry beasts by showing them who they are. They need to understand the difference between them and the hyenas. You have to build their confidence while bringing out aggression from their bones.

Share your blueprint

Experience comes from a lot of years of mistakes. You know what this means if you are a leader. You probably know what should and shouldn't be done to become successful.

This is wisdom you have acquired over time and what your young pros might not understand. They might be pretty and curved, but they might lack the tactics of speaking to the mind and soul of a potential client.

As their mentor, you will need to show them. Let them watch you use the best marketing and selling practices as you work with them. As a result, they will do better without making a lot of mistakes.

Lead and encourage them

We have already talked about hard marketing and selling is. Some of your young lions and lionesses might feel like giving up. They will meet friends who will tell them it is not the right job. It is not worth the effort.

As their leader, those are moments in which your leadership skills come into play. It is for those moments they will remember you. You should be there for them, encouraging them to push through until they achieve what they want.

Provide constructive feedback

I am sure you have heard people say, "It is not what you say, but how you say it." Every leader, whether you are a line manager for some company or your own business, should know how to give constructive feedback.

Constructive feedback does not look at what somebody has done but rather shows someone the other way of doing it. "I understand what you were trying to do, but you should try doing it like this in the future." This statement will help you build teams.

This type of feedback is aimed at building your team for future strong performance. It is not aimed at finding the one at fault or the person who should be punished. Read some leadership books for more about this.

Emphasize the importance of money

I have never worked in a profitable organization that did not emphasize the numbers issue. Business is all about the numbers. The bottom line (profit) depends on the top line (sales).

If you work for an organization where they pay bonuses, you should understand that bonuses come from what the business will make after profit. Therefore, it is important for you to align your teams toward money.

Your team should be able to understand how their performance will affect the performance of the company. They should also understand how it will affect their commissions, salary increments, and bonuses.

Money is at the center of every business. You will be a failure as a leader if your people are not aligned with the importance of money. You should also be a company that rewards good performance with good benefit packages.

Create a contest through targets

In every marketing and selling department, performance reports are shared on a daily, weekly, monthly, quarterly and/or yearly basis.

These reports usually indicate the performance of every person and unit.

What I like about marketing and sales is the ability to tangibly measure the performance of every individual and department. Marketing and sales are not a place where you justify your performance with fluffy statements.

I know that targets are challenging and can sometimes overwhelm people's abilities. But to a larger extent, they are good for both the company and the people who work for it.

The best way to inspire great performance from your teams is by creating a contest with a wonderful prize. As human beings, we always work with our own selfish interests.

Most people will want to be on top if there is a trip to Mauritius, a car to be won, or an instant promotion for a certain vacancy. The advantage to the company is total performance. Targets also help your young lions and lionesses with focus.

Since everyone is doing it for their own selfish reasons, you will have a number of salespeople doing great and pushing the total performance through the roof.

Become their Idol

I know one old woman who had only one son. This woman lost both her husband and son while she was in her late 60s. In Africa, people rarely have savings on which to rely in their old age. I used to wonder how this woman would survive in her late 80s.

It was in 1999 when I asked myself those questions. This woman is still alive and living a normal life without savings. But she had help from the government. Since I was close to her, I asked her how she had been surviving.

And she said, "I am an idol. People like you and your friends come to me for wisdom. And you usually don't come empty-handed."

She explained further, saying, "Our interactions with people should add value. You will only come to me if you are getting something out of me. Therefore, I have decided to give value to young people. In turn, it has helped me to have friends who care about me."

There are young people who provide more value than old people. We also have people who are very old and more valuable than young ones. Jim Rohn once said, "People will pay you for the value you bring to the table."

Understand that naming yourself a CEO without understanding how to acquire clients will make you lose that title sooner than you think. Your business will disappear as a result of ambitious and innovative people having the desire to grow their business.

However, when you decide to collaborate and give value to the young ones, people will come and visit. They hope to receive a blessing. Look at great people like Nelson Mandela and Mother Teresa. People all over the world traveled to meet them.

This kind of respect started from somewhere. These people were known, provided value, inspired others, changed the rules and touched people's lives with their service. It is now time for you to believe in your business.

You need to shamelessly go out there to sell your products and/or services. Upon getting business, remember to give your best service possible. Doing this will improve your repeat business. But most importantly, leverage the new crops of talented salespeople within or outside your company.

And that's how you market and sell like a prostitute!

Thanks for reading. I wish you all the best in your marketing and sales journey.

Edwin.

www.ingramcontent.com/pod-product-compliance
Lightning Source LLC
Chambersburg PA
CBHW021817170526
45157CB00007B/2621